Simplifying Common Assessment

A GUIDE FOR PROFESSIONAL LEARNING COMMUNITIES AT WORK®

Kim Bailey & Chris Jakicic

Solution Tree | Press

a division of

Solution Tree

555 North Morton Street
Bloomington, IN 47404
800.733.6786 (toll free) / 812.336.7700
FAX: 812.336.7790

email: info@SolutionTree.com
SolutionTree.com

Visit **go.SolutionTree.com/assessment** to download the free reproducibles in this book.

Printed in the United States of America

Library of Congress Control Number: 2016952857
ISBN: 978-1-943874-45-3

Solution Tree
Jeffrey C. Jones, CEO
Edmund M. Ackerman, President

Solution Tree Press
President: Douglas M. Rife
Editorial Director: Tonya Maddox Cupp
Managing Production Editor: Caroline Weiss
Senior Production Editor: Tara Perkins
Senior Editor: Amy Rubenstein
Copy Chief: Sarah Payne-Mills
Copy Editors: Miranda Addonizio and Sarah Payne-Mills
Proofreader: Elisabeth Abrams
Text and Cover Designer: Abigail Bowen
Editorial Assistants: Jessi Finn and Kendra Slayton

This book is dedicated to Dr. Richard DuFour: our mentor, our friend, our inspiration, and our conscience in this important work.

ACKNOWLEDGMENTS

This book is the result of many collaborative conversations and reflects our collective learning from many great educators across the years. And we're never done learning. Our work is still influenced by many colleagues who inspire, support, and challenge us. While the list of those individuals is endless and would never truly capture everyone who has contributed to and supported our practice, we would like to specifically thank Rick and Becky DuFour, Jeffrey Jones, Douglas Rife, Mike Mattos, Austin Buffum, Jeanne Spiller, Claudia Wheatley, Shannon Ritz, Tom Many, and Bill Ferriter.

Finally, we have the incredible opportunity to see educators in the field of education take this information and make it their own—this is the most meaningful aspect of our work, and we watch with excitement as they impact the future of all students.

Solution Tree Press would like to thank the following reviewers:

Clint Heitz
Language Arts Teacher
Bettendorf High School
Bettendorf, Iowa

Thomas Kennedy
Assistant Principal
Rocky Mountain
   Middle School
Idaho Falls, Idaho

Craig Mah
Principal
Walton Elementary School
Coquitlam, British
   Columbia, Canada

Matthew Mayer
Principal
Kenneth Murphy
   Elementary School
Beach Park, Illinois

Cory Radisch
Principal
Monmouth Regional
   High School
Tinton Falls, New Jersey

Lee Ann Spillane-Larke
Language Arts Teacher
Cypress Creek High School
Orlando, Florida

Jonathan Vander Els
Principal
Memorial Elementary School
Newton, New Hampshire

Visit **go.SolutionTree.com/assessment** to download the free reproducibles in this book.

TABLE OF CONTENTS

CHAPTER 6

Using Data to Support Student Learning 77

CHAPTER 7

Focusing on Feedback and Grappling With Grading 93

ABOUT THE AUTHORS

Kim Bailey is former director of professional development and instructional support for the Capistrano Unified School District in southern California. Her leadership was instrumental in uniting and guiding educators throughout the district's fifty-eight schools on their journey to becoming professional learning communities. She also taught courses in educational leadership as an adjunct faculty member at Chapman University in Orange, California. Prior to her work in professional development, Kim served as an administrator of special education programs and a teacher of students with disabilities.

Kim's education background spans thirty-nine years, and her work at Capistrano has won national praise. The National School Boards Association (NSBA) recognized Kim's leadership in coordinating and implementing the district's Professional Development Academies. The academies received the distinguished NSBA Magna Award and the California School Boards Association Golden Bell Award. Kim has served on the Committee on Accreditation for the California Commission on Teaching Credentialing.

As a writer and consultant, Kim works with U.S. educators to build effective leadership of PLCs. She is passionate about empowering teams with practical, collaborative strategies for aligning instruction, assessment, and interventions with the standards so all students receive high-quality instruction.

Kim earned a bachelor of science and a master of science in education and special education from Northern Illinois University.

To learn more about Kim's work, visit http://kbailey4learning.wordpress.com or follow @Bailey4learning on Twitter.

Chris Jakicic, EdD, served as principal of Woodlawn Middle School in Illinois from its opening day in 1999 through the spring of 2007. Under her leadership, the staff shifted toward a collaborative culture focused on learning and implemented formative assessment practices to shape their instructional strategies. Student motivation and performance increased. Chris began her career teaching middle school science before serving as principal of Willow Grove Elementary School in Illinois for nine years. At Willow Grove, she helped teachers develop high-performing collaborative teams to increase student learning.

Through her work with teachers and administrators across the United States, Chris emphasizes that effective teaming is the heart of PLCs. She also shares practical knowledge about how to use data conversations to interpret classroom information for effective instruction. She has worked closely with schools and districts that want to use the power of common formative assessments to increase learning for all students. She provides specific, practical strategies for teams who want to make the best use of their limited common planning time to write effective assessments meeting the rigor of the Common Core State Standards. Teams can use the data from these assessments to effectively provide students with exactly what they need next.

Chris has written articles for the *Journal of Staff Development* and *Illinois School Research and Development Journal* detailing her experiences with common assessments and PLCs. She has worked as an adjunct instructor at National Louis University as well as Loyola University Chicago, where she earned a doctor of education.

To learn more about Chris's work, visit www.chrisjakicic.com or follow @cjakicic on Twitter.

To book Kim Bailey or Chris Jakicic for professional development, contact pd@SolutionTree.com.

FOREWORD

By Richard DuFour and Rebecca DuFour

Since 1998, we have written books and articles on the Professional Learning Community at Work process, made presentations to hundreds of thousands of teachers and principals on the topic, and helped educators implement the PLC process in their own schools and districts. In doing so, we have witnessed the often stark differences in the ways educators approach bringing the PLC process to life in their own schools.

Those schools truly committed to transformation engage in an ongoing process of continuous improvement that uses actual evidence of student learning to inform and improve their instructional practice and to better meet the individual needs of each student. They acquire this evidence through a comprehensive assessment process that relies heavily on teacher-made common formative assessments.

Alternatively, schools committed to preserving their traditional structure and culture rather than creating the conditions that lead to higher levels of learning for students and adults, often look for ways to avoid doing the real work of PLCs. They settle for *PLC lite*—they call themselves a PLC, though they avoid doing what PLCs actually do and are thus not truly able to reculture their schools.

In *Simplifying Common Assessment: A Guide for Professional Learning Communities at Work*, authors Kim Bailey and Chris Jakicic challenge educators to use the PLC process, and particularly assessment, as a key strategy for improving student and adult learning—to bolster transformation efforts and reject PLC lite. The authors make the following compelling arguments.

- Assessments can serve as a powerful tool for school improvement if they are part of a larger process to transform a traditional school into a PLC. Educators can create rigorous assessments that would make a psychometrician green with envy; however, if the results from assessments are not used properly, there is no reason to expect higher levels of student learning.

- Unless a faculty is committed to high levels of learning for all students, assessments will be used to report student learning but not to improve it.

- No one person has the energy and expertise to meet all of the learning needs of each student assigned to a classroom. The call to help all students learn at high levels can only be answered through a collaborative culture in which educators work in teams and take collective responsibility for student learning.

- In each unit of instruction the members of the collaborative team must be crystal clear on the knowledge, skills, and dispositions each student is to acquire. Very importantly, they must also agree on what proficiency looks like.

- Systematic interventions that guarantee struggling students receive additional time and support for learning until those students are able to demonstrate proficiency will require concrete evidence of each student's learning in a way that is timely and targeted.

- While struggling students receive additional time and support for learning during intervention time, students who have demonstrated a high level of proficiency on the common assessments benefit from systematic extension of their learning.

- A team's collective analysis of student learning evidence through common assessments serves as a powerful catalyst for instructional improvement because it helps members identify individual strengths to share, individual concerns to address, and areas where no team members have yet to experience success. The team uses that information in shaping its professional development.

- The best assessment process is balanced. It will utilize both ongoing checks for understanding in the classroom each day as well as individual teacher assessments during the unit. There will be a place for both summative and formative assessments, pencil-and-paper and performance-based assessments, and short-term and longer-term assessments.

An assessment process that does not take these factors into account dramatically reduces the impact it has on improving student learning.

A key question that drives the work of collaborative teams in a true PLC is, "How will we know our students have learned? How will we know each student has acquired the essential knowledge, skills, and dispositions of this unit?" This question is meaningful only if there is a commitment on the part of the entire school to ensure that all students become proficient in the essential skills of each unit. If a school is truly dedicated to helping all students learn at high levels, each collaborative team of teachers will study the intended curriculum such as state and national standards and district curriculum guides. Members will then unwrap the standards to clarify more specifically what students should know and be able to do. They will establish common pacing for each unit so the team can gather evidence of student learning during the unit. They will study the rigor and format of the high-stakes assessments and will develop assessments to prepare their students for the rigor of those high-stakes tests. They will describe as specifically as possible what proficient work looks like.

The real test of a true PLC is to determine how each teacher team uses the evidence of student learning its members gather from common assessments. The assessment is directly aligned to essential learnings of the unit. The teams identify which students were unable to demonstrate proficiency on a particular skill. Because the school is dedicated to helping all students learn essential skills and concepts, time has been built into the schedule during the school day to provide these students with additional time and support for learning in a way that does not remove them from new direct instruction. Students will continue to receive this additional support until they have demonstrated proficiency. For the students that have demonstrated proficiency on the common assessment, that same time is used to extend and enrich their learning of the newly acquired skills and concepts.

Teams also use student learning evidence to identify individual teachers' strengths and weaknesses. For example, if common assessments consistently demonstrate your students are better able to demonstrate proficiency than my students, I have an opportunity to learn from you. Teams can devote their collaborative time to sharing members' effective instructional strategies or, if no one on the team is getting good results, can focus on professional development from outside of the team, building, or district personnel to expand their collective ability.

In our decades of work in schools, we have seen the trap of PLC lite in regard to assessment transformation. Teachers within a school culture that is content to merely give students the *opportunity* to learn rather than *ensuring* student learning will see little reason to participate in this collaborative and collective effort. Rather than teams engaging in the essential dialogue of a PLC about what students must learn, the school simply distributes the appropriate grade-level standards and materials others create. Rather than having teams grapple with the "How do we know our students are learning?" question, they use the assessments from the textbook, or take turns writing the assessment, or administer the assessment but only to assign grades. Pacing from class to class varies greatly, so a *system* of intervention and extension is impossible because individual same-grade or same-subject teachers are teaching different skills to different students at different times.

Worst of all, the school loses out on the power of common assessments to reveal individual teacher strengths and weaknesses or curriculum areas where students consistently struggle. Assessment reverts back to a tool for assigning grades rather than a catalyst for improving learning for both students and adults.

To their great credit, the authors of this powerful resource present educators with specific tools for writing good assessments and provide protocols that can help in gathering and analyzing evidence of student learning. They certainly address these important areas in a thoughtful way, and their book will help teams become better at writing assessments and analyzing achievement data. But more importantly, Kim and Chris put assessment in the larger context of the PLC process. They present compelling evidence that our best hope for improving schools is developing the capacity of educators to function as members of a PLC. Furthermore, they demonstrate that unless collaborative teams of teachers are using evidence of student learning from common assessments to inform and improve their instructional practice, they are not yet a true professional learning community.

If you are looking for tools to reinforce teacher isolation and help your school look better as a PLC lite school, this book is not for you. If, on the other hand, you recognize the need for significant cultural shifts in your school and want to learn at a deeper level about how a strong common formative assessment process can facilitate those shifts, *Simplifying Common Assessment: A Guide for Professional Learning Communities at Work* will help you achieve these goals. It is an outstanding addition to the literature on PLCs and has a prominent place in our professional library. It should be in yours as well.

INTRODUCTION

Framing the Power of Assessment in Professional Learning Communities

Several years ago, we were both working in school systems and trying to make sense of our work and its relationship to standards-based instruction and accountability. Some schools searched for a silver bullet to help them reach high standards, and every effort seemed to result in random improvements with little focus on meeting the needs of all students. Then, we got lucky. Even though we worked in different states and had different roles, we were both enlightened by a powerful model for our practice that set the tone for the work we would do in our schools: professional learning communities (PLCs). Its architects, Richard DuFour, Rebecca DuFour, and Robert Eaker, described a model of continual improvement that schools could use to ensure high levels of learning. The idea of a PLC is not simply to meet external accountability measures, nor is it a silver-bullet program. It requires a thorough change in school or district culture.

We learned that schools get better results by shifting their focus from teaching to learning and that, when school staff members work in collaborative teams in a cycle of improvement, they clarify what students should really know and do. And we learned that when teams actually monitor those things, their students learn at higher levels. They don't write off students who aren't achieving those targeted skills and concepts but rather take responsibility for supporting struggling students' needs. And as a result, they ensure all students receive what they have a right to: a powerful education that helps them attain essential skills and concepts they need to prepare them for whatever they choose to do in their lives.

Needless to say, we were all for it. Yet simply embracing the PLC model wasn't enough. We needed to put legs on it—to make it operational within our own systems. Working with our respective colleagues and continuing to grow in our own knowledge, we identified ways we could implement the model and support the work. Because it was one of the more challenging aspects to implement, we focused on strategies for common assessment. We learned from our experiences how difficult writing and using team-designed common formative assessments (CFAs) could be, particularly when dealing with standards that were complex or unfamiliar to all members on a team. In fact, we saw some teams practically paralyzed from moving forward with using common formative assessments for fear they might be doing something wrong. We also observed that some schools and districts take unfortunate shortcuts around this work,

1

like using test bank questions or vendor-produced assessments that weren't necessarily providing teams with meaningful data. Given the frequency of these two observations, we wrote our first book, *Common Formative Assessment: A Toolkit for Professional Learning Communities at Work* (Bailey & Jakicic, 2012), to reflect on what we learned in the process. We intended to provide the protocols and templates that would help collaborative teams design and use common assessments in a very practical way. We designed it to help teams build the confidence to develop assessments that would work more effectively and provide information that would help them increase their students' learning.

Since then, we've had the privilege of working with schools and districts across the United States as they do this important work. We've also worked with experienced teams who've navigated the increased rigor accompanying the Common Core standards (National Governors Association Center for Best Practices [NGA] & Council of Chief State School Officers [CCSSO], 2010a, 2010b) and other state standards. These experiences have enriched our thinking about how collaborative teams can do this work; and we've come to understand some ways that teams can be more efficient as well as more effective. This book lays out these ideas and ways that teams can effectively write and use common formative assessments. For those who have read and used our first book, you'll notice that the process remains the same; however, this book highlights how teams can simplify the process, what works, and what teams should avoid. For those new to writing and using common formative assessments, this book takes you all the way through the process.

Overview of the Process

In education, few terms are more emotionally charged than *assessment*. Merely uttering the word can put students, educators, parents, and the general public on high alert, triggering a range of emotions including nervousness, fear, confusion, and frustration. In reality, the word *assessment* is vague—its meaning encompasses a host of possible types and purposes connected to the term. We can interpret *assessment* to mean different things, depending on the context or nature of the experience and our perspective or personal connection to the process and outcomes.

Richard DuFour, Rebecca DuFour, Robert Eaker, Thomas Many, and Mike Mattos (2016) lay out one of the core beliefs that guide the work of collaborative teams in their book *Learning by Doing*—that is, that teams learn most when they actually get started on the work and then continually reflect and revise throughout the implementation process. We support this principle and encourage teams to get started with the intentional planning process (the *P* in the PDSA cycle—plan, do, study, act), knowing that they will learn as they go. We encourage you to start with the following four steps.

1. Identify the essential standards for your course or grade level.

2. Unwrap standards into learning targets.

3. Pace those learning targets (from the essential standards as well as the supporting standards) throughout the school year.

4. Develop units of instruction that identify when you will give and use common formative assessments.

Those familiar with the big ideas and foundation of professional learning communities can typically recite the four critical questions that guide the work of PLCs (DuFour et al., 2016).

1. What knowledge, skills, and dispositions should every student acquire as a result of this unit, this course, or this grade level?

2. How will we know when each student has acquired the essential knowledge and skills?

3. How will we respond when some students do not learn?

4. How will we extend the learning for students who are already proficient?

Effective collaborative teams work in a cyclical fashion, continually answering these questions in a PDSA cycle for each unit. By first focusing on question 1, What knowledge, skills, and dispositions should every student acquire as a result of this unit, this course, or this grade level?, teams closely examine the essential standards they will be teaching and determine the subset knowledge and skills—in other words, the *learning targets*—that build toward the accomplishment of that standard. This close examination, called *unwrapping* or *unpacking*, ensures clarity for each member of a collaborative team and increases accuracy in the pacing and design of instruction and assessments. While learning targets are generally derived from standards, some less-complex standards may function as a learning target itself. One of the benefits of unwrapping the standards before this work is that teams can focus on individual learning targets instead of the broader standards. The next question, How will we know when each student has acquired the essential knowledge and skills?, is, in our opinion, the most pivotal question we can answer—one that fuels the power of teams. By addressing this question, teams design and use meaningful assessments, making that critical shift from a focus on teaching to a focus on learning. The team focuses on results, keeping assessment data at the forefront of all decisions related to student learning, including teachers' responses when students don't acquire a certain skill or concept (question 3) or require increased challenge or differentiation (question 4). Figure I.1 provides a visual representation of this PDSA cycle and the work teams accomplish within each phase.

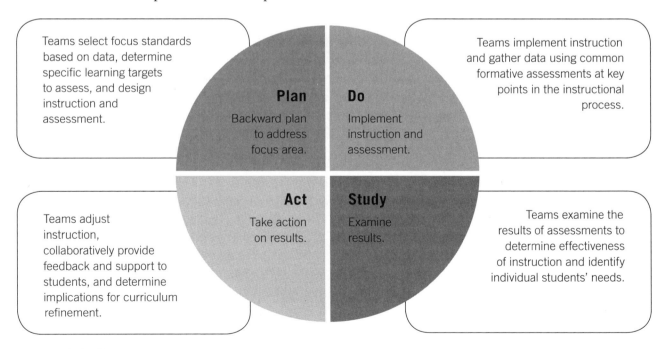

Figure I.1: PDSA cycle.

Getting teams to a point where they are confident working in this cycle takes time and dedication and is not without its challenges, especially with regard to assessment. Recognize that the work will likely not be perfect, but your team will learn a lot about what is important and how to best use information to help students achieve. Throughout the chapters in this book, we provide information teams need to work through these steps to create common assessments to gauge student knowledge, respond to their needs, and ensure all students learn the essential information and skills to ensure their future success.

Overview of Chapters

We continue to believe that schools and districts need a balanced assessment system that includes both formative and summative assessments. We have found that merely labeling an assessment *formative* or *summative* rarely helps teams move forward. Rather, understanding the purpose of the assessment you're writing and using is the key to analyzing the information the assessment provides. We explore these issues in chapter 1, where we lay out our thinking about the types of questions teams can ask for different assessments. As we think about the term *simplify*, we believe that, for assessments, it starts here—understanding why and how a team creates a balanced assessment system with the important components but that isn't unnecessarily overwhelming.

In chapter 2, we help teams navigate their understanding of what their state standards mean and how they can build consensus about what proficiency will look like for students. We discuss the importance of answering the first critical question for collaborative teams: What knowledge, skills, and dispositions should every student acquire as a result of this unit, this course, or this grade level? Teams must identify and come to consensus on the essential standards they will guarantee for all students. We also explore how teams achieve collective clarity about proficiency when they work collaboratively to unwrap these standards.

In chapter 3, we take a more intensive look at rigor than we've previously done in our work. The term *rigor* has become so commonplace in our discussions that we worry it has lost its importance. In this chapter, we discuss how our focus on rigor must influence the work of assessment. In chapter 4, we follow up this discussion by looking at how high-performing teams can effectively align their curriculum, instruction, and assessment to the more rigorous standards they've adopted. We explore topics such as how often to give assessments and how we can find the time in an already jam-packed curriculum to respond to the results.

In chapter 5, we look at strategies for making the process of developing and writing assessments more practical for teachers. We lay out what's important in the process and make sense of specific steps and strategies teams can use to make their assessments more valid and reliable.

We know from our experiences working with teams that understanding how to effectively use the results from assessments is often a confusing step. We know that when teams collaboratively design a quality assessment, it will more easily lead to an effective team response. In chapter 6 we help teams work through this process collaboratively and share three specific strategies for using data to plan effective responses.

We explore issues related to grading and feedback in chapter 7. We discuss the difference between scoring and grading assessments, and how developing a growth mindset for both teachers and students can result in better use of assessment results to guide assessment work.

Finally, in chapter 8, we address the barriers that singleton teachers face when writing and responding to common assessments. We suggest ways vertical, interdisciplinary, cross-school and district, and electronic teams benefit from collaboratively writing quality assessments and responding to the results.

Throughout the book, we provide sample scenarios and note specific school and practitioner names. These names are fictitious, but the examples we provide are based on realities in our own experiences and within the schools and with the teachers we have worked with. For each chapter, we start with a list of the most common questions and challenges we encounter as we work with teams. We anticipate that as you use this book, these are some of the questions you might have heard from others or wanted to ask. These questions will be addressed throughout the chapter. At the end of each chapter, we also provide a section called Tips for Traction. Our purpose for providing these ideas is to help you identify what knowledge and actions will best move you and your team forward. We hope that these tips help you achieve better success and efficiency without taking the shortcuts we've seen others try that can result in skipping some important work.

We've also included an appendix containing an implementation road map for the process of developing and using quality common assessments. By using the road map throughout their journey, teams can identify where they are, progress they've made in their implementation, and what their next steps should be. The goal is to embrace and fully experience this journey—the results are worth it.

CHAPTER 1

Clarifying Assessment Types and Uses

COMMON QUESTIONS AND CHALLENGES

- Why do we have to do all of these assessments? When do we get time to teach?
- What value does each type of assessment bring to the work, and which assessments are the most important to collaborative teams?
- How much time should we spend analyzing data from the various assessments?

Through our work on assessment with schools operating as PLCs, we've become aware of individual teachers' and teams' frustrations regarding the amount of student time required to take certain assessments and teacher time required to analyze the results. If their perception is that these assessments have little useable value, it adds salt to the wound. It's not uncommon to hear educators exclaim, "We spend too much time testing!" or "How can I teach when they keep making us give more assessments? Now they're asking us to do common assessments?" At times, these comments and questions provide us with the impression that teams may be unclear on the purpose and value of each assessment type, which influenced this chapter. We have also noticed that many teams get sidetracked by trying to label assessments as either formative or summative, as though there is only one right type of assessment. We've become convinced that the really critical conversation is about the purpose of the assessment. How will teachers use the results? Being able to match the purpose of the assessment to the data it reveals is much more important than labeling it.

Given the many revisions in state standards and the significant shifts in what we want students to know and be able to do, it stands to reason that we must realign all levels of assessment: state assessments, district benchmark assessments, team-developed common assessments, and classroom formative assessments. To begin examining the role of assessment in collaborative teams, we thought it would be a good idea first to clarify assessment types and the differences between not only their purpose but also the information they provide to improve student learning. We find it important to specifically examine the types of assessment that districts, schools, and classrooms use most frequently, explaining not only the context and purpose of each but the roles that teams take in gathering and using the information. We have categorized the bulk of assessment types into the following three categories.

1. Current (within-unit) assessments

2. Progressive or periodic assessments

3. Cumulative or annual assessments

Table 1.1 outlines examples of more specific assessments for each type.

Table 1.1: Examples of Assessment Types

Current (Within-Unit) Assessments	Progressive or Periodic Assessments	Cumulative or Annual Assessments
• Classroom formative assessment practices • Common formative assessments, including preassessments • Common summative assessments	• Quarterly or trimester benchmarks or interim measures • Periodic progress monitoring of supports and interventions • End-of-course assessments	• State assessments (such as Smarter Balanced Assessment Consortium [SBAC], Partnership for Assessment of Readiness for College and Careers [PARCC], and so on) • Language development assessments

For each assessment category, we discuss the types of information teams derive and provide insight into *wide-angle* and *close-up* questions that teams might ask as they examine data from the assessment results. We refer to *wide-angle questions* as the big-picture questions that schools and teams ask. In a wide-angle view, teams look at their data from a distance and see general trends and patterns as a whole. The conversations focus on questions that uncover general information about student achievement levels, particular areas of strength and concern, and comparisons with prior data. The data at this level can assist districts and teams to examine issues related to the alignment, design, and pacing of curriculum, assessment, and instruction.

Close-up questions, on the other hand, take a closer look at the data. Teams can use these questions to drill down and examine specific groups of students as well as individual students to determine their particular strengths, weaknesses, and progress. Each question type serves an important purpose in the overall work of teams.

Current (Within-Unit) Assessments

Let's start by looking at the types of assessments that are directly connected to teaching on a day-to-day basis. We can classify current assessments conducted within a curricular unit into three main types: (1) unit-based common summative assessments, (2) unit-based common formative measures, and (3) in-class formative assessment strategies.

Unit-Based Common Summative Assessments

Summative unit assessments directly tie to the day-to-day instruction that teams deliver. They answer the question of whether all students master the skills and concepts teams want them to achieve by the end of the instructional unit. Teams can use common summative assessments to improve the alignment of the taught curriculum, help identify students still not achieving the targeted level of mastery for essential standards, and reveal any major skills and concepts that teams should emphasize in future units.

Summative assessments cumulatively measure the learning targets that teams teach throughout the unit. Teacher teams design these assessments during their instructional unit planning. In that critical planning phase, the team identifies the skills and concepts that students should know and do, and collectively agrees on the types of tasks that accurately measure whether students have attained them. The content of the assessment should prioritize those skills and concepts deemed most essential and should align to the level of rigor sought in the standards. Teams should format assessment items in a similar fashion to the item types students will likely encounter in their state assessments.

Table 1.2 provides the wide-angle and close-up questions answered when teams examine results from these assessments. The questions relate to three major areas: students' *achievement*, the *alignment* of their instruction and curriculum, and implications for any *assistance* their students may need. In wide-angle fashion, the team first analyzes overall patterns in their students' achievement and identifies key learning targets that they need to carry forward and reinforce in future instruction. They identify any alignment issues and implications for changing their pacing or instructional approaches. In close-up fashion, they pinpoint specific students who need further support to master the essential standards that the unit targets.

Table 1.2: Questions Teams Answer With Unit-Based Common Summative Assessments

	Wide-Angle Questions	Close-Up Questions
Achievement	What was the overall performance of students on this measure? Did our students meet the expected levels of proficiency?	Are there any concepts or skills we should carry forward in our instruction as we teach and assess in the next unit?
Alignment	Did we intentionally teach the skills and concepts we targeted in our original plan? Do the essential standards we selected align with those we prioritize in the assessment?	How might these results inform the design of our instruction the next time we teach this unit?
Assistance	How are student subgroups performing in relation to the majority of students? Are there clusters of students significantly above or below the targeted performance levels?	Are any students not consistently demonstrating progress toward mastering the foundational or essential skills we identified? Did we provide these students additional scaffolding or support as we taught the unit? What was the response to this support?

Unit-Based Common Formative Measures

The type of assessments we feel hit the sweet spot for teams regarding information and relevance are common formative assessments. In their pivotal work *Learning by Doing*, DuFour et al. (2016) share the power and purpose of common formative assessments that teams design and administer throughout the year. They describe that through these common assessments, teams can:

> identify and address program concerns (areas of learning where many students are experiencing difficulty). They also examine the results to discover strengths and weaknesses in their individual teaching in order to learn from one another. Very importantly, the assessments are used to identify students who need additional time and support for learning. (DuFour et al., 2016, p. 27)

By design, these administered assessments target the priorities for learning that teams have defined within a unit of study. Their immediate purpose is to monitor each student's mastery of targeted skills and concepts during that unit of study so that he or she can receive support during the instructional process. As a secondary purpose, teams collectively examine student evidence of learning to identify a cause-and-effect relationship between the instructional strategies used and their impact on student learning. By using data from these assessments with both purposes in mind, teams harness the real power behind common formative assessments. The results are relevant and timely, help teams and students to adjust course now (not later), and play a pivotal role in the PDSA process. We believe that common formative assessments are the most visible type of assessment for teachers and students. The data they yield link directly to the current content teachers are teaching their students. They provide immediate feedback on their students' achievement as well as the effectiveness of their instruction. See table 1.3.

Table 1.3: Questions Teams Answer With Unit-Based Common Formative Measures

	Wide-Angle Questions	Close-Up Questions
Achievement	What specific areas of learning did this assessment target? What was the standard for proficiency? In general, how did our students perform on this assessment? Were there common errors or misconceptions?	How did specific students perform on this unit assessment? Were there students achieving above or below expectations?
Alignment	Did our instruction seem to align to the targeted learning? What potential gaps in our instruction might account for areas of weakness? What skill sets or standards did we design the assessment to measure?	Did we design our instruction to lead to proficiency on these targets? What implications for our instructional design come from these data?
Assistance	What students or groups demonstrate significant gaps in their achievement on this assessment?	Which specific students need additional assistance? How might we strengthen the areas we identified from the results of this assessment for specific students?

In-Class Formative Assessment Strategies

The most immediate data teachers have at their fingertips are the day-to-day information pieces gained through in-class formative assessment strategies. Frequently called *checks for understanding*, these practices can effectively support high levels of student learning. In general, individual teachers implement these. There are two types of checks for understanding: (1) those that produce a temporary or fleeting snapshot of student learning and (2) those that create a *permanent product*, in other words, something concrete or tangible that can be brought to a team meeting and discussed. Each type has its advantages and applications in the classroom.

Effective teachers constantly gather information on the fly to ascertain student understanding as they provide instruction. Using probing questions or other brief strategies such as red light, yellow light, and green light cards, thumbs up or down, or student responses on a whiteboard, teachers can gain insight into students' level of understanding of certain concepts or their ability to perform a certain task. However, to truly know where individual students are in their learning, teachers must intentionally and systematically implement in-class formative assessments. Using only on-the-fly or nonpermanent strategies may help determine whether most students understand as teachers deliver instruction, but it is difficult to pinpoint which specific students aren't getting it and their strengths, missteps, or misconceptions without a *tangible product*—something that can be seen and discussed later. For example, it's practically impossible to capture specific information about each student's understanding based solely on the use of thumbs up or down. While the strategy provides teachers a sense of student understanding during a lesson, it's momentary and can't fully capture information about which students understood—or how well they understood—the information or process.

We share this information as a reminder. In our work, we see far too often that teachers and teams rely on their momentary checks for understanding rather than collecting clear evidence of student learning through a more tangible product. Formative assessment using tangible products can also serve as common formative assessments, and the team can collaboratively design and plan how it will use them. For example, individual teachers frequently use exit cards as a means to check their students' understanding. Exit cards provide a tangible product that enables teachers to see what their students are thinking, or how well they understand a particular concept. If a team collaboratively designs the prompt of this exit card to monitor a specific learning target and each teacher gives the same prompt in his or her class, teachers can bring their cards to their next meeting and collectively look at the results. This dual purpose eliminates the need for every teacher to design his or her formative assessments independently. It's part of the "working smarter, not harder" attitude that underlies the work of collaborative teams. It also ensures that the assessments we design are more likely to be aligned and accurate measures of what we consider essential in student learning. In chapter 5, we will describe how to design these more informative and specific assessments in a meaningful and doable fashion. Table 1.4 provides the questions that can be answered using in-class formative assessment strategies (note that because these are implemented on an individual classroom basis, we only include close-up questions).

Table 1.4: Questions Teachers Answer With In-Class Formative Assessment Strategies

	Close-Up Questions
Achievement	Am I seeing evidence that students understand the concept I am teaching? Is there evidence of student demonstration of the skill being taught?
Alignment	Do I need to spend more or less time teaching this concept or skill?
	Do I need to break this concept or skill into smaller parts to ensure my students learn?
Assistance	Do there seem to be any misconceptions I need to undo?
	Do any students seem to be struggling with this concept or skill?
	Are there any students who already know this?

Progressive or Periodic Assessments

We can conduct progressive or periodic assessments through (1) district benchmark assessments and (2) content-specific progress-monitoring tools.

District Benchmark Assessments

Rather than miss an opportunity to impact learning before the comprehensive state assessments, many educational systems seek interim sources of data. Districts and schools frequently design or purchase assessment tools to monitor student progress toward the end-of-year standards. These benchmark assessments are formal interim measures administered periodically during the instructional year and are often designed to emulate a smaller version of the state assessment. The intent of these assessments is often twofold: (1) to provide students with an experience similar to the end-of-year or state assessment and (2) to serve as universal screening tools that can provide feedback on group and individual students' progress toward meeting annual learning goals. These assessments can furnish some predictive insight into the outcomes and, when used well, can help districts, schools, and teams adjust their courses regarding curriculum emphasis, targeted interventions, and monitoring of areas they identify as potential gaps.

On a wide-angle basis, teams can use the information to monitor and adjust upcoming instruction in specific areas of the curriculum to ensure their students are making appropriate progress toward the goals. They can then use the results to identify students in need of additional support. To make the most of benchmark assessment information, teams need to understand how they are designed. For example, some benchmarks align with a district pacing guide to measure students on skills they have presumably learned. Other tools are more comprehensive in nature, requiring students to respond to some items that assess information that they have not yet learned. The design of the assessment has implications for how we use the information or data. If the assessment measures what we have already taught, then the data may reveal areas that we need to revisit.

On a close-up level, teams can examine information from benchmark assessments for individual students or student groups, revealing areas of strength and weakness within particular skill sets that can be targeted for supplemental reinforcement, reteaching, or focused interventions. As a universal screening, teams can compile this information to develop watchlists, inform intervention programs, and reveal specific learning gaps for individual students.

While still considered summative in nature, benchmark assessments can tie more directly to what teachers taught in the curriculum, particularly if they disaggregate data to provide information about student proficiency in specific learning targets. However, teams often find it challenging to use the results in a meaningful way because they have begun teaching the next set of learning targets in their yearlong curriculum. A common theme we hear among teachers is that the further from day-to-day instruction the assessment information arrives, the less meaningful the information tends to be and the less likely teams are to gain significant insight to inform their daily instruction.

Content-Specific Progress-Monitoring Tools

Many districts have elected to use key assessments to monitor student progress in literacy and numeracy skills. Sometimes these tools are called *curriculum-based measures* and focus on a select set of skills and concepts deemed appropriate for certain grade bands. Typically found at the elementary level, these assessments serve as both benchmark assessments and tools to monitor progress. Quite often, teachers use the results as universal screening tools to ensure that students progress at expected levels in specific literacy areas. For example, the DIBELS Data System tracks students' levels of performance and rates of improvement so teams can make "data-driven, timely decisions and improve student outcomes" (University of Oregon, n.d.). Teams can use information coming from this type of assessment to provide differentiated and individualized instructional support and gather feedback on how it's working. They should monitor the performance and development of literacy skills for all students who are at risk of reading difficulty. Teams can use the data they gather during progress monitoring in their instructional decisions. See table 1.5 for questions that both benchmark and content-specific progress-monitoring tools can help teams answer.

Table 1.5: Questions Teams Answer With Content-Specific Progress-Monitoring Tools

	Wide-Angle Questions	Close-Up Questions
Achievement	How did all students perform on this assessment? What was the standard for proficiency?	How did specific students perform on this benchmark? How did students who attended specific programs or interventions perform?
Alignment	On what standards or skill sets did we assess students in this benchmark? What potential gaps in our instruction might account for areas of weakness?	What implications for our instructional design for the next portion of the year come from these data? Are there skills we need to address more intentionally?
Assistance	What students or student groups demonstrate significant gaps in their achievement on this assessment?	Which students need additional assistance? Are students who are not demonstrating proficiency receiving the amount and type of support that they need? Do we need to make adjustments? How might we strengthen the areas we identified from the results of this assessment for specific students?

Cumulative or Annual Assessments

At the same time they published the standards, the authors of the Common Core State Standards (CCSS) explicitly outlined the need and rationale for assessments that differ substantially from those teachers used with prior standards—ones that more effectively measured the types of knowledge and skills the standards highlighted and emphasized instructional shifts. Two assessment consortia serve several U.S. states in this endeavor: Smarter Balanced Assessment Consortium and Partnership for Assessment of Readiness for College and Careers. The remaining states have elected to work independently of the two consortia and have designed custom state assessments, generally in partnership with assessment publishers.

State assessments are summative in nature, and their purpose is to measure the annual status of students' mastery of standards identified for a specific course or grade level in grades 3–12. They reflect student performance of targeted skills and concepts in a testing context, and they most often use digital tools across sessions ranging from a total of approximately seven to ten hours in length. As part of this comprehensive assessment, several states also embed a performance task requirement within the same window of time. In this type of task, students may be required to read and analyze information from a number of sources, answer questions and support their answers with evidence, and write a response to a prompt related to information they read.

It's no surprise that the results from state assessments are the most visible pieces of data, including to the public. We see the results in newspaper headlines, we wait with bated breath to see how our schools and districts performed, and parents desperately seek specific information about how well their children achieved. As practitioners, we believe there is value in establishing a consistent apples-to-apples measure of the annual goals. In our personal observations, we have seen evidence that the SBAC and PARCC assessments are better aligned to measure the intended curriculum defined by the standards than they were in the past. This observation gives us hope that teams will use the results in a more productive fashion—not to narrow the taught curriculum but rather to deepen it and support the shifts the standards outline. We believe that this type of high-stakes assessment is a moment-in-time measure of everything that we have emphasized (hopefully) and targeted for mastery during the year of instruction.

So how might PLCs use information coming from these assessments? First, let's look at the big picture or wide-angle view of the data. Teams can examine the information to gauge the comprehensive alignment of the taught curriculum. In other words, districts, schools, and teams should ask the questions, "Did students learn what they needed to learn? Did we teach the skills and concepts measured on the assessment? Do we see significant disconnects or areas of misalignment?" Looking at the data in a close-up view, teams can identify and monitor the achievement of specific students, including English learners, students with disabilities, and economically or ethnically diverse students. Likewise, the data can reveal nonidentified students who demonstrate significant lags in their achievement. Teams should also ask questions such as, "What subgroups are showing significantly different levels of achievement?"

Despite the fact that high-stakes state assessments have been revised to better reflect the standards, some teams are not yet fully aware of the specific content and skills they measure or the expectations for mastery they hold. To collectively clarify and gain insight on dispositions, skills, and strategies that students must demonstrate on these state assessments, teams can examine released items or examples from the assessments. Then they can translate these insights into instructional plans that build these strategies over time. For example, upon seeing the complexity and length of texts that students must read within the context of the assessments, teams can intentionally build students' endurance and abilities over time by increasing the amount of text they're reading independently throughout the year. By studying items and analyzing specific standards or clusters, teams can also identify strengths and areas of need based on the prior year's achievement. When teams identify gaps or areas that they need to address more effectively within the curriculum, they can take action and redesign their instruction.

Wide-angle and close-up questions, categorized into the topics of achievement, alignment, and assistance, also allow teams to get the most from annual assessments (see table 1.6). Districts benefit from analysis that gauges the overall levels of student proficiency. However, state assessments should not be the only type of assessment data that districts and teams seek. While they provide big-picture information, they are insufficient as tools to provide the meaningful and accurate information teams need to drive instructional design and targeted interventions.

Table 1.6: Questions Teams Answer With Cumulative or Annual Assessments

	Wide-Angle Questions	**Close-Up Questions**
Achievement	What was the overall performance of students in each grade level or course?	How did specific subgroups perform? How did students who attended specific programs or interventions perform? Did the gap close?
Alignment	What potential gaps in our instruction might account for areas of weakness? Is our written curriculum aligned to both the content and the rigor of the emphasized standards? Do the essential standards we selected align with those we prioritized in the assessment?	Does our taught curriculum align to both the content and the rigor of the emphasized standards? What implications for our instructional design come from these data?
Assistance	How are student subgroups performing in relation to the majority of students? Are there clusters of students significantly above or below the targeted performance levels?	Who specifically needs assistance? Are there students not previously identified who require urgent support? In which specific clusters or skill sets do our identified students need assistance?

Conclusion

Regardless of the assessment type, we know that we achieve meaning and momentum when we effectively collaborate on many levels: between teachers on a grade-level or content team, in vertical or multiple content teams, and even between students and teachers. Understanding the purpose and guiding questions for each type, however, can facilitate more purposeful conversations and productive outcomes within that collaboration. As you read this book, we will expand on key elements within the overall process of working with common assessments and provide specific protocols that engage team members and students to productively analyze their results.

TIPS FOR TRACTION

- Get clear on the purpose and focus of each assessment type. Keep these in mind when examining results and making decisions about instruction and support.

- As a team, spend the most time focusing on the design and use of assessments that directly impact your instruction—in other words, your common summative and formative assessments. By ensuring that your instruction and assessment align to the standards and using the PDSA cycle to guarantee that all students master the most essential skills throughout each unit of study, your team will set the stage for success on the summative assessments as well as annual or cumulative assessments.

CHAPTER 2

Starting With the End in Mind

COMMON QUESTIONS AND CHALLENGES

- What are essential standards, and how do we use them in our work?
- Do we really need to unwrap the standards? What form should we use? Doesn't this take time?
- Can we use documents that show us the already unwrapped standards?
- Do we design assessments for the standards or the learning targets?
- How do we build other skills into our assessments, such as digital literacy?

Robert J. Marzano's (2003) research shows that the number-one factor for successful schools is a curriculum that is the same for all students, no matter which teacher they're assigned, and having enough time to adequately teach that curriculum. He refers to this as a *guaranteed and viable curriculum*.

Before teams can effectively design their instruction and assessments to ensure a guaranteed and viable curriculum, they need to clarify their outcomes for student learning. In his book *The 7 Habits of Highly Effective People*, Stephen Covey (2012) calls this the *end in mind*—to start with a clear understanding of the destination. In the context of designing quality instruction and assessments, being clear about the end in mind means that members must agree on the knowledge, concepts, and information that their students will have, and the skills or performances students demonstrate by the end of instruction.

To achieve this, we focus on the first critical question of a PLC: What knowledge, skills, and dispositions should every student acquire as a result of this unit, this course, or this grade level? This question sounds simple, and the answer may seem obvious—in fact, we often hear the response, "We've already got our list of standards!" Because of that perceived simplicity, teams often gloss over that question. Members might assume that everyone *gets* what the standards ask. And while they may indeed have their list of standards or even a smartphone app that outlines what students will learn, unless every teacher sitting at the table shares expectations for his or her students' learning and agrees on the evidence that will show that they've actually learned it, there is little chance that all students will learn the same essential skills and concepts with a similar level of rigor. This inequitable outcome certainly runs counter to the guiding principle that all students should receive a guaranteed and viable curriculum.

It's important for every team member to share clarity about the end in mind for student learning—team members cannot simply assume that they all have the same picture of success. They must verify it. In order for teams to achieve this clarity about what their students should know and be able to do, they must identify the essential standards they want students to master, unwrap those standards to decipher the learning targets contained within each, and begin establishing how the learning targets align and overlap so they can arrange them within instructional units. In this chapter, we share effective strategies that teams can use to build that common clarity quickly and efficiently. These strategies will lay the foundation for designing effective and aligned instruction and assessments.

Determine the Essential Standards

Before designing and using assessments, teams first need to determine what they will prioritize in their teaching. To some, this step may seem redundant or even unnecessary given the widespread belief that we simply focus our teaching on the standards. While that is true, we need to look at the magnitude of that statement and the reality of time available in traditional schools.

Let's look at the facts. Depending on the grade level, there are between seventy-three and ninety-one English language arts (ELA) standards in the CCSS (NGA & CCSSO, 2010a). Across the typical forty weeks of schooling our students attend (not taking time out for other activities such as field trips), we would have to tackle a minimum of two standards each week (and the students would have to master them). Yet teachers now know that many standards subsume multiple learning targets (subskills and concepts); students don't achieve them in a *one and done* fashion. Because the standards seek a deeper level of learning, they build student knowledge and skill over a long period of time, not simply one week.

Now let's add the mathematics standards to the equation (NGA & CCSSO, 2010b). In grades K–8, we see a range of twenty-five to forty-seven standards that we need to address. However, just as we see in the English language arts standards, there are multiple learning targets subsumed within each of these standards.

The bottom line is that, given our time limits, we cannot realistically guarantee every one of these standards for every student, and we cannot teach everything to the depth necessary for conceptual understanding. We can, however, filter the list of standards to those that we know are essential to teach, assess, monitor, and support when students have not yet mastered them. If we want our students to build conceptual understanding and deepen their learning, we need to decide which standards are truly essential versus those that we might de-emphasize. Teams must place their collaborative focus on those that are most essential.

This filtering process does not imply that the other standards disappear from the curriculum. Rather, we de-emphasize them in terms of specific monitoring and interventions. If a school district hasn't yet completed this filtering, we suggest that sites structure the time and process for their teams to examine and prioritize their curriculum. This process can be done all at once during the first few collaborative team meetings of the school year, or teams can determine these essential standards unit by unit throughout the year. Teams that have engaged in this work find that making time to teach, assess, and provide corrective instruction becomes more manageable. Additionally, when grade-level as well as vertical teams agree about learning priorities, school teams raise the likelihood that students will arrive to the next grade level or course more adequately prepared.

Different districts and schools use various terms like *essential standards*, *power standards*, *emphasized standards*, and *priority standards*. Regardless of the term, they typically all refer to what Larry Ainsworth (2010) describes as:

> A carefully selected *subset* of the total list of the grade-specific and course-specific standards within each content area that students must know and be able to do by the end of each school year in order to be prepared to enter the next grade level or course. (pp. 39–40)

In other words, these prioritized standards comprise the guaranteed and viable curriculum that students will receive.

Numerous districts determine their essential standards by having teacher teams use three major filters to examine each standard to determine the most important (Reeves, 2007).

1. **Readiness:** This concerns the prerequisite skills for future learning without which students would be unsuccessful. For example, students in grade 5 would need to know how to add, subtract, multiply, and divide fractions in order to be prepared for the work of applying fractions in grade 6.

2. **Leverage:** Skills with *leverage* are powerful and applicable across a number of content areas. For example, the skill of summarizing is crucial in all content areas. To illustrate this point, students must be able to identify and communicate key points and relevant supporting details to more briefly retell literary stories, condense events and influences in history, and write concise conclusions in a lab report.

3. **Endurance:** Skills we consider to be enduring refer to those that students will use throughout their school, career, and life situations. Skills that relate to number sense or estimating, for example, enable students to determine whether a mathematical solution makes sense.

Ainsworth (2013) also recommends that teams consider a fourth filter: *external exams*. These are concepts and skills that students are most likely to encounter on annual standardized tests, college entrance exams, and occupational competency exams.

The process starts with each teacher reviewing the standards for his or her curriculum and looking for those that meet these criteria. Once each teacher has made this initial determination, the team builds consensus about which standards should make the draft list. Teams should prioritize standards according to the blueprints and information provided about them. For example, PARCC's Model Content Frameworks contain major clusters for mathematics in grades K–8. These clusters refer to standards that require greater emphasis than the others based on the depth of the ideas, the time that they take to master, and their importance to future mathematics or the demands of college and career readiness. In short, they are the essential mathematics standards for the particular grade level.

When each team has reached consensus on the standards it believes are essential, the school or district should provide time for all teachers to ascertain whether they have a vertically aligned set of standards. For example, if grades 1, 2, and 3 have each independently determined a similar standard is essential, teams want to ensure that they aren't being redundant and that they are actually integrating the heightened complexity reflected in their grade-level standards and building on the skill progression from grade to grade.

Consider the grade-level progression of standard 9 in Reading Standards for Informational Text:

- **Grade 1:** Identify basic similarities in and differences between two texts on the same topic (e.g., in illustrations, descriptions, or procedures). (RI.1.9)

- **Grade 2:** Compare and contrast the most important points presented by two texts on the same topic. (RI.2.9)

- **Grade 3:** Compare and contrast the most important points and key details presented in two texts on the same topic. (RI.3.9)

Note that students in grade 1 will be identifying basic similarities and differences between two texts on the same topic, while students in grade 2 will need to identify the most important points and then compare and contrast them.

After these skills are identified, the team then agrees to write and use a common formative assessment to make sure all students are proficient. Having teams talk vertically helps make sure all teachers are aware of which standards are essential in each course or grade.

The essential standards serve as a foundational hub around which teams conduct all of their collaborative work. It is important that all teachers, students, and parents understand what the essential standards are and how they will be used. This is one way to begin involving students in the assessment process, and it also ensures that parents understand what's most important for their children to know.

Once teams identify the essential standards, they will refer to them throughout the PDSA cycle. In chapter 4, we discuss how teams move from essential standards to pacing guides and then, finally, to units of instruction. When they plan a unit of study, teams refer to the essential standards to ensure that they're prioritizing the right standards within the unit. They will also discuss strategies to support the quality instruction of the essential standards. They will commonly design assessments based on the essential standards to make sure their students can demonstrate them with an agreed-on level of mastery. Finally, when they collectively examine their common assessment results, teams determine which students need further support in the essential standards.

In *Collaborating for Success With the Common Core: A Toolkit for Professional Learning Communities at Work* (Bailey, Jakicic, & Spiller, 2014), we introduce a four-step process for identifying and reaching consensus on essential standards. We have provided this protocol in figure 2.1 as a tool that teams can use at either the district or site level.

To answer the first question a collaborative team asks (What do we want our students to learn?), the team identifies power or essential standards. This protocol provides a step-by step process to do this work.

Preparation

1. Make sure the team is familiar with the three appendices for the ELA standards and appendix A for the mathematics standards and have copies on hand.

2. Each team member will need a copy of the grade-level or course standards the team is powering, and a copy of the standards for the grade level before and the grade level after or the course before and the course after.

3. Teams will use chart paper to write the initial draft list of the standards.

4. Provide copies of sample items (or whole test blueprint, if available) from PARCC or SBAC for each team.

5. The team should review what the criteria (endurance, leverage, and readiness) mean.

6. The team should review all of the grade-level standards to see how they are organized.

Process

- **Step One:** Identify potential power standards using the filtering criteria. Each teacher privately reads the standards and identifies which standards he or she believes should be a power standard.

- **Step Two:** Develop a first draft based on team members' recommendations. The team works to build consensus on which standards should be powered for specific grade levels or courses.

- **Step Three:** Determine alignment between draft power standards and other related documentation. The team considers PARCC and SBAC documents and reviews any data or test blueprints that provide information about which standards should be given more priority.

- **Step Four:** Review for vertical alignment. All of the teachers review all of the standards on the draft list vertically, to see if there are gaps or redundancies. A final list of power standards for the school or district is compiled.

Figure 2.1: Protocol for powering the Common Core.

Source: Bailey et al., 2014.

Visit **go.SolutionTree.com/assessment** *for a free reproducible version of this figure.*

Unwrap the Standards

In *Common Formative Assessment: A Toolkit for Professional Learning Communities at Work* (Bailey & Jakicic, 2012) and *Collaborating for Success With the Common Core* (Bailey et al., 2014), we outline the process of *unwrapping* that guides teams through a structured conversation designed to get to the heart of the standards. We also share that there are variations of terms used for this process (for example, teams may be familiar with *unpacking* or *deconstructing* the standards). In general, whatever term is used, or slight differences in the process, the overall goal is the same. The goal of the unwrapping process is twofold: first, to build shared or collective understanding of what the standard asks students to know and do; and second, to identify the smaller increments of learning, or learning targets, that will create a step-by-step path leading to that standard.

In its simplest form, we use the unwrapping process to examine a single standard and identify the smaller learning targets it contains. The standard may explicitly state these learning targets, yet it may imply others. In some cases, a standard may have only one learning target. For example, consider the first-grade standard "Identify who is telling the story at different parts of the text" (RL.1.6; NGA & CCSSO, 2010a).

This process doesn't need to take a lot of team time. Once teams have gone through it a couple of times, it's possible to conduct an unwrapping conversation in ten minutes or less. The key is to still have that conversation, however, and not assume that everyone on the team is familiar with the content of the standards or pictures the same end in mind for student learning. While it's tempting to skip over the process to start the more lively conversation about instructional strategies and lesson activities, we promise that the unwrapping process is powerful, sharpening team focus and ensuring clarity that carries forward in all subsequent discussions. Whether you use the template sample we have provided or you have another way to document the learning targets, we suggest compiling them in a notebook (digital or physical) organized by units. Each year, teams can reference the work they've already done. Doing so means that teams can refine and revise the process as necessary instead of starting from scratch.

We get many questions about the available online documents and tools that have already unwrapped the standards into learning targets. While we agree that these tools might serve to jump-start the conversation about addressing the standards in a particular unit of study, we strongly believe that they cannot replace the conversation. In our observation, some of the tools, although well intended, contain gaps or overly simplistic interpretations of the standards and don't represent their full essence. It all comes down to this: teams should use their professional judgment. They should read any documents that purport to have done all of the work of teams with a critical eye. They should accept nothing as perfect, and team members should always have the chance to talk through the learning targets, question anything that doesn't make sense, and edit anything they don't believe is fully aligned or appropriate.

Steps of the Unwrapping Process

To begin the unwrapping process, ensure each team member has a copy of the standard under examination or can work together to view the standard using a document camera or writing on poster paper. We find that a simple template helps to organize the process and guide the conversation. See figure 2.2 for a template. The template can be projected and viewed by the team as one member takes notes on a computer or completed while standing around the poster. If preferred, members can each have a paper copy of the template and complete them during the conversation. We suggest that one person serve as the official recorder in this instance to make sure that all thoughts are noted.

Standard to address			
Context or conditions (What text, problem type, or situation will students encounter?)			
Learning Targets		**Depth of Knowledge**	**Assessment**
Concepts or information students need to know (including big idea)	Big idea:		
Skills students will demonstrate			
Academic language and vocabulary			

Figure 2.2: Unwrapping template.

Source: Adapted from Bailey et al., 2014.

*Visit **go.SolutionTree.com/assessment** for a free reproducible version of this figure.*

Teams work through four steps as they unwrap the standard together and enter information into the unwrapping template.

Step 1: Annotate the Standard

In our observation, annotating the standards spotlights key concepts and skills within the standard. It also reveals information about the nature or context of the tasks students will encounter. Teams will find that by completing this simple act of highlighting the standard, they jump-start collective clarity about its intent and focus. It sets the stage for outlining specific learning targets, which is the next step of the process. The process usually takes less than a minute and ensures that everyone on the team focuses on the content of the standards. In other words, it's a minute well spent!

Teams should record the standard in question in the top row of the template (*Standard to address*). If each teacher on the team is recording on his or her own copy of the template, he or she would follow along and do the same process. Following are descriptions of a common annotating system teams can use.

- **Put brackets around any information in the standard that tells about the context:** Context may refer to the type of text students will read, the type of problem that students will solve, or any other situational information about the nature of the challenge or task students should encounter as they demonstrate their understanding of key concepts and skills. Consider this example of an eighth-grade geometry standard (NGA & CCSSO, 2010b).

   Apply the Pythagorean Theorem to determine [unknown side lengths in right triangles] in [real-world and mathematical problems] in [two and three dimensions]. (8.G.B.7)

   We have placed brackets around information that clarifies that students must be given right triangles with unknown side lengths in two and three dimensions, and the problems they're given should be authentic or real-world problems.

- **Circle the verbs:** Doing so points to the main skills we expect students to do or demonstrate. We've demonstrated this highlight with the words *apply* and *determine*.

   Apply the Pythagorean Theorem to determine [unknown side lengths in right triangles] in [real-world and mathematical problems] in [two and three dimensions]. (8.G.B.7)

- **Underline the significant nouns or noun phrases:** These words help point to the concepts, definitions, facts, or ideas that students will need to know or understand. In this example, the underlined words help us know that students should understand the term and concept of the Pythagorean Theorem, know a strategy for finding unknown side lengths, and understand how to apply the strategy in two- versus three-dimensional right triangles.

   Apply the Pythagorean Theorem to determine [unknown side lengths in right triangles] in [real-world and mathematical problems] in [two and three dimensions]. (8.G.B.7)

Step 2: Collectively Identify the Specific Learning Targets That Reflect What Students Will Know and Do

To jump-start the process of answering the first critical question "What would our students need to know and do in order to accomplish this standard?" and filling in the *Learning Targets* column in the template, use the circled and underlined words that we highlighted in step 1. During this process, teams should not only use these highlighted words but also read between the lines and add any concepts or skills that the standard implies but doesn't explicitly state. These are crucial *knows* and *dos* when students successfully complete the task.

While the standard doesn't explicitly state anything about students demonstrating these in-between steps, when teams fill in the blanks, they ensure the appropriate design of instruction and assessments that will lead to high levels of student learning. When identifying the knows, be sure to include any concepts that support the standards' big idea or main objective. Some teams add a special place in their templates to house the big idea, as shown in the template in figure 2.2 (page 22).

Step 3: Identify Any Academic Language or Vocabulary That Students Should Master

Teams can reference not only the words they underlined when they highlighted the standard but can also examine their list of learning targets to determine any other terms that they should intentionally teach and assess. Teams should see redundancy between this list of words and their learning targets.

Step 4: Examine the Rigor of the Learning Targets

Using a common language, examine the learning targets (the knows and dos) to determine the level of rigor and complexity. For common language, we recommend Norman Webb's (1997) Depth of Knowledge (DOK), which is referenced in a number of standards-based documents throughout the United States. While chapter 3 goes into further detail about the role of DOK in assessment, we thought it appropriate to provide a brief summary here.

This tool enables educators to analyze the standards and identify the level of complexity or cognitive demand of that standard—in other words, the depth of knowledge to be demonstrated by the learner. Once the targeted depth of knowledge is clear to teachers, it is easier to identify and align assessments and instruction. There are four levels of DOK.

1. **Recall and reproduction:** Tasks that ask students to identify or recall facts, processes, or terms

2. **Skills and concepts:** Tasks that go beyond basic recall and require students to apply knowledge, such as to interpret information, show cause and effect, or classify

3. **Strategic thinking and reasoning:** Tasks that could have multiple correct answers and require the learner to reason at a higher level, including nonroutine problems or testing and supporting a hypothesis

4. **Extended thinking:** Tasks that require integrating information from multiple sources and solving problems with unpredictable solutions

While teams can examine the verbs in the learning targets, we caution that if they use verbs alone, they may cause misunderstanding about the actual intended rigor in the learning target. We, along with others (Aungst, 2014; Hess, 2008), recommend that teams examine what comes after the verb as well as the context (which was bracketed in step 1) to fully understand the expected level of knowledge processing. For further information on how teams examine rigor, see chapter 3.

Figure 2.3 provides an example of the template after teams have finished all four steps. Note that this template provides space to record particular assessment items that will measure the learning targets teams have identified during the unwrapping process. Because this step occurs after the unwrapping process, we have left that column blank in our example.

Standards to address	[Apply] the Pythagorean Theorem to [determine] [unknown side lengths] in [right triangles] in [real-world and mathematical problems] in [two and three dimensions]. (8.G.B.7)		
Context or conditions (What text, problem type, or situation will students encounter?)	Use real-world problems in which there are unknown side lengths in two- and three-dimensional right triangles.		
Learning Targets		**Depth of Knowledge**	**Assessment**
Concepts or information students need to know (including big idea)	• Pythagorean Theorem and instances to use it (Big idea: We use the Pythagorean Theorem to find a missing side length in right triangles only.)	DOK 1	
	• The elements of leg and hypotenuse in the context of a right triangle	DOK 1	
	• Considerations for working with two- versus three-dimensional figures	DOK 2	
Skills students will demonstrate	• Identify the legs and hypotenuse in a right triangle.	DOK 1	
	• Identify the right triangle in a three-dimensional figure.	DOK 1	
	• Analyze the information in a real-world problem that incorporates right triangles with unknown sides.	DOK 3	
	• Apply the Pythagorean Theorem to solve the problem in a two-dimensional figure.	DOK 2	
Academic language and vocabulary	*hypotenuse* *leg* *Pythagorean Theorem* *square root*		

Figure 2.3: Sample unwrapped standard.

Unwrapping Standards for Mathematical Practice

Another dimension of the CCSS for mathematics is the Standards for Mathematical Practice, which describe targets for how students interact and grow mathematically. Mathematics instruction expects that students will not only learn specific content but will also grow in these eight practices (NGA & CCSSO, 2010b).

1. Make sense of problems and persevere in solving them.

2. Reason abstractly and quantitatively.

3. Construct viable arguments and critique the reasoning of others.

4. Model with mathematics.

5. Use appropriate tools strategically.

6. Attend to precision.

7. Look for and make use of structure.

8. Look for and express regularity in repeated reasoning.

As teams unwrap the standards to identify what they want students to know and do in mathematics, they should continually reference the Mathematical Practices. These standards contain the big picture for students: helping them become mathematical thinkers and problem solvers.

We should see evidence of these practices within the work our students produce, demonstrate, and communicate. Given this importance, teams should ensure their integration in conversations about standards and their assessment.

Consider Multiple Learning Targets Within a Unit of Study

Just as the scope and rigor of our academic standards have been enhanced to ensure that students are ready for college and careers, the end in mind for student learning has become far more dimensional. In *Collaborating for Success With the Common Core* (Bailey et al., 2014), we assert that there are consistent themes in the standards regardless of the content area. The focus is no longer solely on the retrieval of information, facts, dates, and lists. The Common Core and other state standards place heightened emphasis on effectively investigating information from a variety of sources, using that information to inform new learning, and applying the learning in the context of real-world problems.

While in the past standards tended to resemble a checklist of skills and concepts, we would describe the new considerations for teaching and learning as more closely resembling a Rubik's cube. This often means that learning targets transcend subject-area divisions and apply to several different standards. Teams must negotiate these as they plan units of instruction and budget the time they have throughout a year to cover all the targets for their essential standards. Given that complexity, the need for collaborative conversations and collective clarity across a grade-level or course team has never been greater. Generally, teams approach these conversations as they plan a unit of study. We suggest that teams not only examine the emphasized content standards but also collectively envision the type of task students will be able to perform by the end of the unit of study. Will they be able to solve a specific type of problem? Create a product? What does that look like? With what level of rigor? By first envisioning the ultimate end in mind, teams will better be able to think of the learning targets that progressively enable students to complete that task. It helps to create the instructional journey. The following scenarios illustrate teams negotiating these items.

The fourth-grade team at Chadwick Elementary School in California begins to design its unit on the Southwest Native Americans. They examine their state's social studies standard:

> HSS 4.2.1. Discuss the major nations of California Indians, including their geographic distribution, economic activities, legends, and religious beliefs; and describe how they depended on, adapted to, and modified the physical environment by cultivation of land and use of sea resources. (California Department of Education, 2000, p. 13)

Once the teachers unwrap the standard and define specific information they want their students to know and do, they outline the following learning targets.

- Students will know how California Indians used legends to explain natural phenomena and religious beliefs.

- Students will be able to recall the type of money Native Americans used.

- Students will be able to cite how the local Native Americans adapted to the land and made use of the resources.

While the Chadwick team members did indeed look closely at their social studies standard, they missed an opportunity to make connections to other skills and concepts that are prioritized within fourth grade.

To further explore how a team can expand its impact, let's look at another approach from a fourth-grade team at Castillo Elementary. This team approaches the initial discussion in a similar fashion—first looking at the social studies standard and quickly unwrapping it to reveal specific learning targets. The team's list of knows and dos looks much like the one that the Chadwick team developed. However, as the Castillo team reflects on learning targets, teachers note that they expect students to simply recall information. They realize that the language the standard uses is somewhat vague. They examine the phrase "discuss the major nations of California Indians" (California Department of Education, 2000, p. 13). One could interpret this phrase in many ways. They also note that the phrase "describe how they depended on, adapted to, and modified the physical environment by cultivation of land and use of sea resources" (California Department of Education, 2000, p. 13) is equally vague. They recognize that they want students to take a journey within the unit that builds on their ability to research, read, and analyze informational text, and pull information from quality sources using digital tools. They want students to effectively communicate their learning of the unit's big ideas by writing with a level of quality targeted in fourth grade. They also want to emphasize their ongoing focus on student accountability during collaborative academic conversations.

Based on these considerations, the team grows the focus of the unit from one of students simply regurgitating information to one in which students build their ability to seek information, collaborate, and communicate. We depict the team's thinking process as it develops its plan in figure 2.4.

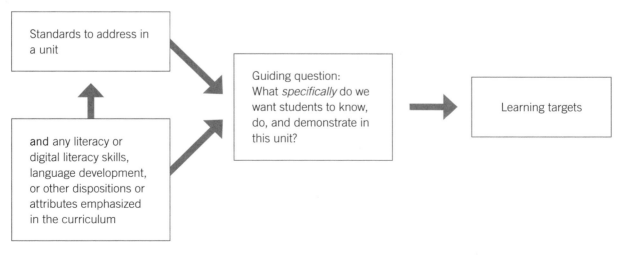

Figure 2.4: Team thinking process for unit design.

Let's see how the team expanded their focus on the essential standards for the unit.

- Discuss the major nations of California Indians, including their geographic distribution, economic activities, legends, and religious beliefs; and describe how they depended on, adapted to, and modified the physical environment by cultivation of land and use of sea resources. (HSS 4.2.1; California Department of Education, 2000, p. 13)

- Refer to details and examples in a text when explaining what the text says explicitly and when drawing inferences from the text. (RI.4.1; NGA & CCSSO, 2010a)

- Explain events, procedures, ideas, or concepts in a historical, scientific, or technical text, including what happened and why, based on specific information in the text. (RI.4.3)

- Write informative or explanatory texts to examine a topic and convey ideas and information clearly.

    a. Introduce a topic clearly and group related information in paragraphs and sections; include formatting (such as headings), illustrations, and multimedia when useful to aiding comprehension.

    b. Develop the topic with facts, definitions, concrete details, quotations, or other information and examples related to the topic.

    c. Link ideas within categories of information using words and phrases (such as another, for example, also, because).

    d. Use precise language and domain-specific vocabulary to inform about or explain the topic.

    e. Provide a concluding statement or section related to the information or explanation presented. (W.4.2)

- Conduct short research projects that build knowledge through investigation of different aspects of a topic. (W.4.7)

- Recall relevant information from experiences or gather relevant information from print and digital sources; take notes, paraphrase, and categorize information, and provide a list of sources. (W.4.8)

As a result of this conversation, every team member is now focused on the comprehensive picture of student learning, one that extends beyond the recall of the content they originally sought. The teachers discussed and envisioned the end in mind for students in a way that integrated the standards, not simply listed them. This clarity set the stage for the design of a unit that intentionally guides students to attain these learning targets within a meaningful context.

If they viewed this list of standards as separate items, the team might have become overwhelmed. However, the teachers were able to quickly categorize the nature of each standard in order to see the whole versus simply seeing the parts. They found that they could easily link and layer the standards. When they examined them as a whole rather than separately, they defined a specific task or product for students to complete, the subset skills of that task, and the qualitative nature of the completed task. Table 2.1 illustrates how teams can organize the standards to assist understanding and integration.

By examining standards addressed within a unit as a whole, teams will more easily design the unit instructional plan and the embedded assessments. And, by expanding their sights on what students should know and do beyond the basic standards, they will set the stage for a richer learning experience for their students.

Table 2.1: Organizing Standards for Understanding and Integration

What Product or Process? (Context of task)	What Content?	How? (Subskills)	With What Quality?
Write informative or explanatory texts to examine a topic and convey ideas and information clearly. (W.4.2)	Information on Southern California tribes, including their geographic distribution, economic activities, legends, and religious beliefs; description of how [tribes] depended on, adapted to, and modified the physical environment by cultivation of land and use of sea resources (HSS 4.2.1)	Introduce a topic clearly and group related information in paragraphs and sections; include formatting (e.g., headings), illustrations, and multimedia when useful to aiding comprehension. (W.4.2a) Develop the topic with facts, definitions, concrete details, quotations, or other information and examples related to the topic. (W.4.2b) Link ideas within categories of information using words and phrases (e.g., *another, for example, also, because*). (W.4.2c) Use precise language and domain-specific vocabulary to inform about or explain the topic. (W.4.2d) Provide a concluding statement or section related to the information or explanation presented. (W.4.2e)	Refer to details and examples in a text when explaining what the text says explicitly and when drawing inferences from the text. (RI.4.1) Explain events, procedures, ideas, or concepts in a historical, scientific, or technical text, including what happened and why, based on specific information in the text. (RI.4.3)
Refer to details and examples in a text when explaining what the text says explicitly and when drawing inferences from the text. (RI.4.1) Conduct short research projects that build knowledge through investigation of different aspects of a topic. (W.4.7)	Information on Southern California tribes	Recall relevant information from experiences or gather relevant information from print and digital sources; take notes, categorize information, and provide a list of sources. (W.4.8)	With appropriate details, sequence, and accuracy

Source: NGA & CCSSO, 2010a.

Work Vertically

As school teams build common clarity around what students should know and be able to do within a particular course or grade level, they should strongly consider examining expectations from a *vertical perspective*—in other words, examining expectations for student learning from one grade to the next and so on. Teams can gain many insights when they examine the end in mind in a vertical fashion. First, by reviewing the standards that come before and after a specific grade level, they shed light on the progression of learning. Second, by gathering input from other grade levels, particularly the one that students will attend after a team's current grade, they expand their awareness and group accountability for learning.

For example, an elementary school might vertically examine the Common Core Writing strand using the following five steps (NGA & CCSSO, 2010a).

1. **Preparation:** The school first determines the focus standard of the vertical progression. For example, it may select anchor standard one for writing: "Write arguments to support claims in an analysis of substantive topics or texts, using valid reasoning and relevant and sufficient evidence" (CCRA.W.1). This anchor standard defines the end in mind for students to be prepared in the area of writing to the point that they are ready to succeed in college and workforce training programs. Each grade-level set of standards in writing progressively contributes to the accomplishment of this anchor standard. So, as part of this activity, each grade-level or course team would plan to examine its grade-specific standards that make up the progression to that anchor standard, as follows.

   Use a combination of drawing, dictating, and writing to compose opinion pieces in which they tell a reader the topic or the name of the book they are writing about and state an opinion or preference about the topic or book (such as *My favorite book is . . .*). (W.K.1)

   Write opinion pieces in which they introduce the topic or name the book they are writing about, state an opinion, supply a reason for the opinion, and provide some sense of closure. (W.1.1)

   Write opinion pieces in which they introduce the topic or book they are writing about, state an opinion, supply reasons that support the opinion, use linking words (such as *because*, *and*, *also*) to connect opinion and reasons, and provide a concluding statement or section. (W.2.1)

   Write opinion pieces on topics or texts, supporting a point of view with reasons. (W.3.1)

   Produce clear and coherent writing in which the development, organization, and style are appropriate to task, purpose, and audience. (W.4.1)

   Write opinion pieces on topics or texts, supporting a point of view with reasons and information. (W.5.1)

   In this example, a fifth-grade team would examine standard W.5.1, the sixth grade team would examine W.6.1, and so on.

2. **Grade-level unwrapping:** To examine the learning targets for its students, each grade-level team unwraps its corresponding standard, using poster paper as a template to indicate the learning targets and academic language related to its particular standard.

3. **Round 1 poster walk:** Each team participating in the activity then walks around viewing the posters that each grade level displays. We suggest having each grade-level team start at the grade level that comes *after* its grade since teachers will be preparing students for the next level of learning. In other words, they will see their role in establishing a strong foundation for the next grade-level learning. Using sticky notes, teachers can point out significant shifts in the expectations they see in the unwrapped standards, ask questions about something they've seen, or suggest additions to the learning targets. See figure 2.5 for a sample of what a fifth-grade team's poster with unwrapped targets might look like.

4. **Round 2 poster walk:** In a second round, grade-level team members should go to the poster of the grade level *preceding* theirs to make special notations on specific learning targets that would be crucial to master. For example, the fifth-grade team could closely examine the fourth-grade

poster and place an asterisk by the skills that teachers feel would enable students to hit the ground running when they transition to fifth grade.

5. **Learning reflection:** After some talk time, each grade-level or course team takes turns reporting its learning from the vertical experience to the rest of the teams, sharing any patterns they might have seen as the standards progressed from grade to grade, any potential implications for their instruction and assessment based on this new knowledge, and specific actions they will take. The entire group collectively charts a summary of actions.

Grade 5 Standard: Write opinion pieces on topics or texts, supporting a point of view with reasons and information. (W.5.1)	
What do we want students to know?	• Know that the purpose of an opinion piece is to express a point of view but support that point of view with reasons and opinion • Know that logical arguments are based on facts that support the author's opinion
What do we want students to do?	• Establish their opinion statement • Identify specific and relevant reasons that support their opinion • Identify potential opposing viewpoints • Group and order the information in a logical way for writing • Compose a written opinion
What academic language will be emphasized?	• Argument • Opinion • Perspective • Persuasive technique • Point of view

Figure 2.5: Sample unwrapped targets for a grade 5 standard.

Schools can hold other vertical conversations that focus on a number of topics, including:

- Expectations for writing quality
- Text-complexity examples by grade level
- Lab report expectations
- Standards for Mathematical Practice

We strongly encourage schoolwide vertical conversations such as these to deepen teams' understanding of the standards' intent, prioritize essential learning targets and academic language that students will master, and establish collective responsibility for students' attainment of the progression of skills during learning.

Conclusion

This chapter has highlighted strategies for teams to use as they develop a common picture of the end in mind for student learning—from determining essential standards to unwrapping the standards for teams to address in a unit of study. The demands of more rigorous standards and the necessary skills to succeed in college and career frame this discussion. Chapter 3 expands the conversation on rigor and provides strategies for teams as they ensure alignment with the expectations of a challenging curriculum.

TIPS FOR TRACTION

- Don't just jump into unwrapping. First, clarify the essential standards.

- Picture the end in mind for the unit of study. Use that picture of success to incrementally identify what students should know and do.

- Use the power of vertical teams to examine a strand within the ELA standards or cluster within the mathematics standards as they progress from one grade to the next. Through the process of vertical unwrapping, each grade-level team will see not only how the standard evolves from grade to grade but the crucial role each grade level plays.

CHAPTER 3

Considering Rigor and Complexity

- What is rigor?
- How do we know how challenging to make our assessments?
- What if our students can't do the assessments?
- How can our team know if our assessments match the level of rigor found in the standard?

Given its emphasis within the standards, and its presence within the high-stakes assessments, we've decided to devote an entire chapter to the topic of rigor. Misconceptions abound about what rigor is and isn't, how teams should use information about rigor, and the implications for designing quality assessment items. We hear a common reaction when teachers examine especially rigorous tasks: "Our kids will never be able to do this!" We suggest adopting a *growth mindset* about this work, a term made familiar by the work of Carol Dweck (2008) in her book *Mindset*. Dweck (2008) describes individuals with a *fixed mindset* as those who believe that intelligence and talent are static or fixed traits. Those with a *growth mindset* believe that, with hard work and effort, they can develop their ability and talent. Further, Dweck (2008) discusses the power of *yet* when facing challenging problems—a concept we advise teams to embrace. Maybe our students can't do this . . . yet. The reality is, perhaps our expectations and instruction haven't empowered our students to get there yet. However, if we know the destination is different, we've got to figure out how we're going to get our students there. Several elements contribute to making this happen: we must build students' muscles to ensure they can meet rigorous challenges, recognize the rigor of standards and targets, ensure assessment items align with the targeted level of rigor, and involve students in the assessment process. Before exploring these elements in depth, it's important that teams first gain a deeper understanding of the role rigor plays in the standards.

Identify the Role of Rigor in the Standards

The key impetus behind the standards and related assessments was that previous standards hadn't consistently reflected the level of rigor necessary to effectively prepare students for college and careers. In many cases, state standards and assessment methods focused largely on either recalling information or on low-level skill application, often isolated from any meaningful context. The National Center for Research on Evaluation, Standards, and Student Testing (CRESST) declares that "essential capabilities for 21st century competence . . . heretofore have been grossly underrepresented in most state tests" (Herman & Linn, 2013, p. 5).

Therefore, the CCSS focus on going beyond simply memorizing information and emphasize problem solving and real-world application of skills and concepts. In fact, the very introduction to the CCSS specifically states that one of the criteria is to include "rigorous content and application of knowledge through higher-order skills" (NGA & CCSSO, n.d.a). Within the description of the mathematics standards, rigor refers to:

> Deep, authentic command of mathematical concepts, not making math harder or introducing topics at earlier grades. To help students meet the standards, educators will need to pursue, with equal intensity, three aspects of rigor in the major work of each grade: conceptual understanding, procedural skills and fluency, and application. (NGA & CCSSO, n.d.d)

Increased rigor is also inherent within the standards for literacy:

> Rather than focusing solely on the skills of reading and writing, the ELA/literacy standards highlight the growing complexity of the texts students must read to be ready for the demands of college, career, and life. The standards call for a staircase of increasing complexity so that all students are ready for the demands of college- and career-level reading no later than the end of high school. (NGA & CCSSO, n.d.c)

Clearly, the game changed, and with it the need to adjust all levels of assessment. Starting with annual assessments, SBAC and PARCC frame their item design with specific claims to ensure that assessment items would specifically align with the higher-level thinking skills. See table 3.1.

Table 3.1: SBAC and PARCC Higher-Level Thinking Skills

	Smarter Balanced Assessment Consortium	Partnership for Assessment of Readiness for College and Careers
Mathematics	1. **Concepts and Procedures:** Students can explain and apply mathematical concepts and interpret and carry out mathematical procedures with precision and fluency. 2. **Problem Solving:** Students can solve a range of complex, well-posed problems in pure and applied mathematics, making productive use of knowledge and problem-solving strategies. 3. **Communicating Reasoning:** Students can clearly and precisely construct viable arguments to support their own reasoning and to critique the reasoning of others. 4. **Modeling and Data Analysis:** Students can analyze complex, real-world scenarios and can construct and use mathematical models to interpret and solve problems.	1. **Major Concepts and Procedures:** Students solve problems involving the major content for grade level with connections to practices. 2. **Additional and Supporting Concepts and Procedures:** Students solve problems involving the additional and supporting content for their grade level with connections to practices. 3. **Expressing Mathematics Reasoning:** Students express mathematical reasoning by constructing mathematical arguments and critiques. 4. **Modeling Real-World Problems:** Students solve real-world problems engaging particularly in the modeling practice. 5. **Fluency:** Students demonstrate fluency in areas set forth in the content standards in grades 3–6.

	Smarter Balanced Assessment Consortium	Partnership for Assessment of Readiness for College and Careers
English Language Arts	1. **Reading:** Students can read closely and analytically to comprehend a range of increasingly complex literary and informational texts. 2. **Writing:** Students can produce effective and well-grounded writing for a range of purposes and audiences. 3. **Reading:** Students read and comprehend a range of sufficiently complex texts independently. 4. **Research and Inquiry:** Students can engage in research and inquiry to investigate topics and to analyze, integrate, and present information.	1. **Reading:** Students read and comprehend a range of sufficiently complex texts independently. 2. **Writing:** Students write effectively when using and analyzing sources. 3. **Research:** Students build and present knowledge through research and the integration, comparison, and synthesis of ideas.

So how do assessments meet these objectives? The high-stakes assessments that states use challenge students with a variety of tasks that require significantly more critical thinking and applied problem solving. And students don't simply need to get the "right" answer but identify potential solutions based on complex evidence, justifying and supporting their conclusions or solutions. Let's look at a fourth-grade example of an SBAC performance task in mathematics in which students receive the following tables of information: zoo ticket prices, snack shop menu with prices, gift store prices, the ages of Anna's family members, and a total dollar amount that the family can spend. Students receive a blank table to complete using the information provided. Students are correct when they reflect any combination of food and drink choices and their total costs for each person in the family. Students get the following five questions related to the data:

1. Use the Zoo Ticket Prices table and Anna's Family list to answer the question. What is the total cost, in dollars, of zoo tickets for Anna's family?

2. Use the Snack Shop Menu and Anna's Family list to answer the question. Each person in Anna's family will buy one food item and one drink. Choose one food and one drink item for each person.

3. Use the Snack Shop Menu and Anna's Family list to answer the question. Based on your response in Part A, what is the total cost, in dollars, of the food and drinks for Anna's family?

4. Grandma says they will spend the remaining money at the gift store. How much money, in dollars, is remaining after the family buys zoo tickets, food, and drinks? (Remember they started with $100.)

5. Use the Gift Store Prices table to answer the question. Anna and Ray go into the gift store. Grandma says there are 2 rules for choosing what to buy:

   ◦ Do not buy more than one of any gift.

   ◦ You must buy at least two gifts.

   In your answer, you must have the following:

   ◦ Tell which gifts Anna and Ray can buy.

   ◦ Explain why there is enough money for the gifts you choose.

   (American Institutes for Research, 2013, pp. 3–7)

To successfully complete this task, students will not only need to comprehend the information the charts provide, interpret the question the prompts ask, analyze data on several levels, and apply their knowledge at a variety of levels but must also work progressively with the information provided and reference it as well as solutions to previously answered questions. Unless they accurately calculate the amount of money already spent on zoo tickets, food, and drinks (question 4), students won't get the correct answer to question 5, which is based on the amount of money remaining.

Although we might agree that our students would ultimately benefit from the challenge presented in this type of task, it requires preparation and intentional planning to ensure students learn the skills and develop the endurance to perform these more rigorous tasks.

Build Student Muscles

A common New Year's resolution is to get healthy—eat right, exercise more, cut out unhealthy habits, and so on. These are noble resolutions, but many people fall flat, only to repeat them again and again, year after year. The reality is that many people don't know where to begin and don't have a specific plan for getting from their current reality (sedentary lifestyle, unhealthy eating) to their target. They might get overwhelmed or simply not have the skills. They might begin by trying to run a distance far too rigorous for their current fitness level and feel defeated. We see similar practices when teachers face the challenge of teaching their students to successfully tackle challenging tasks. Many teachers don't know where to begin and are discouraged because they believe their students will be unable to demonstrate success.

However, those who succeed in their fitness journey approach the process systematically. They set small goals that build on each other, they build muscles that will support the tasks they will do, and they monitor and get feedback on their progress. We think that the same approach can work in our teaching. We can examine the long-term goals and then establish smaller goals that students can attain with support. We can build the muscles, or skills, for which students might not have experience or exposure, and we can monitor and provide feedback throughout the process. In other words, rather than being discouraged, we can take on the challenge and set the stage for student success. If we are going to ask students to compare or integrate information from multiple sources, we need to build this ability throughout the curriculum. We can't wait until the *big one*—in other words, the high-stakes assessments used at the end of the year to require students to complete these rigorous tasks. We need to practice along the way and intentionally design our instruction assessments. When designing instruction, teams can create an instructional journey that leads to the targeted level of thinking or cognitive rigor. Let's look at the three steps teams might take to approach their design.

Step 1: Set the Destination

Teams need to be clear on the level of rigor or complexity they seek in their students' thinking and performance by the end of the year. For example, a mathematics team might map out the type of problem, a history or social-science team might examine the type of analysis and evaluation using primary-source documents, a grade-level team may examine the type of text, and an English team might examine the level of writing. Regardless of the course or grade level, end-of-year targets come from clearly identifying the content students will know as well as the depth of knowledge about that content that students will demonstrate. Teams can enhance this information by examining essential standards and pacing guides for the grade level or course.

Step 2: Map Out the Skills Journey

In this step, teams create a sequence for introducing, practicing, and integrating the skills students will learn. For example, if students will complete a performance task that includes analyzing the prompt, teachers must specifically teach, provide opportunities for practice, and assess students' ability to analyze a prompt. In mathematics, a sixth-grade team might need to increase student dialogue in mathematics classes so students can explain and justify their solutions while solving a problem. Figure 3.1 provides an example of how the mathematics team might build students' skills in justifying their solutions. The team uses a common model of scaffolding, moving from modeling, reviewing exemplars, and practicing justification responses to simple problems. As students build proficiency in these skills, teachers facilitate their work with peers as they apply the indicators of quality to anonymous work and then their own work. Teachers give students multiple opportunities to practice within assessments that now use more complex problems. Finally, the teachers remove supports and expect by the end of the year that students will be able to perform the skill independently and meet the expectations for quality. See figure 3.1 for an illustration of how the supports might progress for justifying solutions in mathematics.

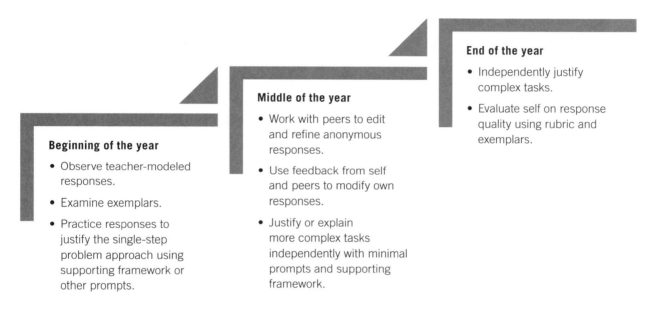

Figure 3.1: Building students' skills throughout the year.

Figure 3.2 is a template that teams can use to discuss the progressions that lead to students' development of major skills they need to successfully complete rigorous, complex assessment items, and to create a plan for expectation, support, and practice (ESP). Teams can use this template to define the gradual increase of expectations over time, the support or specific scaffolds that they will provide to students to meet those expectations (which should decrease over time to ensure independence and automaticity), and the specific opportunities for practice they will integrate in the body of instruction.

Targeted skill	Unit ____	Unit ____	Unit ____	Unit ____	Unit ____
Expectation					
Support					
Practice					

Figure 3.2: Template for building skills throughout the year.

Following are some skills we feel are worthy of building through explicit instruction and scaffolded support.

- Unpacking a prompt
- Citing evidence
- Solving multistep word problems
- Comparing and contrasting
- Developing an argument
- Analyzing data from multiple sources
- Organizing information

Figure 3.3 provides an example of how a team may plan out its incremental expectations across multiple units. This example details an ESP plan for a sixth-grade writing standard (W.6.1.a–e; NGA & CCSSO, 2010a):

Write arguments to support claims with clear reasons and relevant evidence.

Introduce claim(s) and organize the reasons and evidence clearly.

Support claim(s) with clear reasons and relevant evidence, using credible sources and demonstrating an understanding of the topic or text.

Use words, phrases, and clauses to clarify the relationships among claim(s) and reasons.

Establish and maintain a formal style.

Provide a concluding statement or section that follows from the argument presented.

Targeted skill	Unit 1	Unit 2	Unit 3
Expectation	Students will set the stage for the argument by introducing their claim in the first section of a piece, and clearly outline specific reasons for that claim.	Students will identify information that supports each reason, referencing clear citations and evidence. They will begin to use effective transitions to connect and clarify their ideas.	Students will write using effective techniques to support their claim, using credible sources, clear citations, and effective language.
Support	Ensure knowledge about purpose of argumentation writing. Provide opportunities for students to examine claims in various pieces of writing. Debrief characteristics and indicators of effectiveness from examples.	Have students examine effective and ineffective argumentation to identify how well an author supported his or her claims. Students can work in teams to note the word choices that authors use, and the quality of support. Students can make recommendations for improvement.	Using peer review process, have students use feedback on how they supported their claims to edit and make improvements to their work.
Practice	Students will examine examples of well-constructed arguments, and identify strategies for introducing claims.	Students will identify support for specific claims in their argument and practice using clauses that show relationships (for example, *for instance, however, although*).	Students will create arguments incorporating prior knowledge and, using peer feedback, make edits to their work to increase the quality.

Figure 3.3: Example of completed template for building skills throughout the year.

Additionally, the Institute of Education Sciences (IES) identifies the following key recommendations for building muscles in mathematics:

Recommendation 1.

Prepare problems and use them in whole-class instruction.

1. Include both routine and non-routine problems in problem-solving activities.
2. Ensure that students will understand the problem by addressing issues students might encounter with the problem's context or language.
3. Consider students' knowledge of mathematical content when planning lessons.

Recommendation 2.

Assist students in monitoring and reflecting on the problem-solving process.

1. Provide students with a list of prompts to help them monitor and reflect during the problem-solving process.
2. Model how to monitor and reflect on the problem-solving process.
3. Use student thinking about a problem to develop students' ability to monitor and reflect.

Recommendation 3.

Teach students how to use visual representations.

1. Select visual representations that are appropriate for students and the problems they are solving.
2. Use think-alouds and discussions to teach students how to represent problems visually.
3. Show students how to convert the visually represented information into mathematical notation.

Recommendation 4.

Expose students to multiple problem-solving strategies.

1. Provide instruction in multiple strategies.
2. Provide opportunities for students to compare multiple strategies in worked examples.
3. Ask students to generate and share multiple strategies for solving a problem.

Recommendation 5.

Help students recognize and articulate mathematical concepts and notation.

1. Describe relevant mathematical concepts and notation, and relate them to the problem-solving activity.
2. Ask students to explain each step used to solve a problem in a worked example.
3. Help students make sense of algebraic notation.

(Woodward et al., 2012)

These recommendations assist teams as they design instruction that empowers students. When they incorporate these guiding principles into instruction and monitor their development through targeted formative and summative assessments, they can see their students develop those muscles. A free practice guide is available to download from the IES website (Woodward et al., 2012).

Step 3: Establish Intentional Checkpoints

We all know that we can't assume students are moving forward as they develop particular skills; we must incorporate meaningful and aligned formative and summative assessments to chart those movements. For each step along the way, our assessments should include items that measure students' application of the concepts and skills they are learning.

Recognize the Rigor

With past standards, we tended to speak of rigor in vague terms. For some, the term meant *difficult* or *hard*, and for others, it meant that the work was complicated or overly challenging. Some teachers might have even thrown the term around as a badge of honor, claiming that their curriculum was rigorous. The reality is that without a common picture or description of cognitive rigor, it is difficult to determine whether the instruction truly targets the desired level of thinking. For example, if a standard asks students to analyze in detail a series of events described in a text, teacher A might interpret it to mean that students will simply recall a sequence of events. Teacher B, on the other hand, might interpret that same standard to mean that students will examine the relationship between key events, including any relevant causal effects. Unless their teachers engage in a conversation focused on identifying the level of thinking or processing knowledge the standard requires, students in those two classrooms will experience very different levels of rigor based on their teachers' interpretations of the standard.

When teams examine the notion of cognitive rigor, they must consider two aspects. First, they need to recognize the complexity of the task, and second, they must identify the complexity of the stimulus within the task.

Complexity of the Task

While teachers frequently use Bloom's taxonomy as a common language to describe the type of thinking they target, it does not describe levels of complexity or depth. Team members might agree that they want their students to analyze or evaluate information, but might not have a clear picture of what that could look like. This is where Norman Webb's (1997) DOK model has been helpful. He designed the model to examine cognitive expectations in standards, activities, and assessment tasks (Webb, 1997). DOK descriptors reference the complexity of mental processing necessary to answer a question, perform a task, or generate a product. For example, is a particular task asking students to routinely apply a skill, or does it require completing a multistep process to analyze or evaluate the viability of an argument (Hess, Carlock, Jones, & Walkup, 2009)? The DOK model examines and distinguishes the cognitive expectation or depth of knowledge across four levels.

- Level 1 tasks focus on recalling information or using basic processes or formulas. In literacy, for example, students demonstrate level 1 knowledge when they answer literal comprehension questions from a passage of text, such as "Who were the characters in the story?" In mathematics, students would demonstrate level 1 knowledge if they were able to calculate a basic equation or measure the length of an object. Students can either reproduce or recall information or perform basic tasks at this level, which is relatively automatic, with minimal transfer of information required.

- Level 2 tasks require students to go beyond the basic recall or automatic use of information and apply some analytical process to classify, compare, or convert information from one form to another. Within these tasks, students work with the information to make decisions of one type or another.

- Level 3 tasks make knowledge processing more abstract or complex. They require learners to reason and exhibit higher-level critical thinking to address nonroutine problems. Tasks that fall into this category might have more than one possible solution, and would require students to evaluate and justify their actions.

- Level 4 tasks require learners to address complex concepts through in-depth analysis and synthesis of multiple tasks over an extended time period. In these tasks, students are likely using information from multiple sources and potentially creating new information based on evidence. Because of their in-depth nature, level 4 tasks are more time consuming, and often constitute a culminating activity or summative performance task.

Table 3.2 provides a summary of these four levels, including sample tasks for each.

Table 3.2: Depth of Knowledge Task Levels

Level	Description	Sample Tasks
Level 1 **Recalling**	The subject-matter content at this particular level usually involves working with facts, terms, or properties of objects. It may also involve use of simple procedures and formulas. There is little transformation or extended processing of the target knowledge required by the tasks that fall into this category.	Multiply two numbers. Find the area of a rectangle. Convert scientific notation to decimal form. Measure an angle. Write a brief outline and explain the event, process, or story. Write a summary report of the event. Prepare a flowchart that illustrates the sequence of events. Paraphrase a chapter in the book. Retell in your own words. Outline the main points.
Level 2 **Basic Reasoning**	Basic reasoning includes the engagement of some mental processing beyond recalling or reproducing a response. This level generally requires students to contrast or compare people, places, events, and concepts; convert information from one form to another; classify or sort items into meaningful categories; or describe or explain issues and problems, patterns, cause and effect, significance or impact, relationships, points of view, or processes. (If the knowledge necessary to answer an item does not automatically provide the answer, it is at least a level 2. Most actions imply more than one step.)	Classify or organize information. Estimate. Make observations. Collect and display data. Compare data. Apply routine procedures or tasks (such as applying a simple set of rules or protocols to a laboratory situation the same way each time). Explain the meaning of a concept or explain how to perform a particular task. State the relationships among a number of concepts or principles.
Level 3 **Strategic Thinking and Complex Reasoning**	Items falling into this category demand a short-term use of higher-order thinking processes, such as analysis and evaluation, to solve real-world problems with predictable outcomes. Stating one's reasoning is a key marker of tasks that fall into this particular category. (Level 3 is complex and abstract. If more than one response is possible, it is at least a level 3 and calls for use of reasoning, justification, and evidence as support for the response.)	Classify the actions of the characters in a book. Conduct an investigation to produce information to support a view. Write a letter to the editor. Prepare and conduct a debate. Write an argumentative speech arguing for or against _____. Prepare a case to present your views about _____. Explain or work with abstract terms and concepts.

continued →

Level	Description	Sample Tasks
Level 4 **Extended Thinking**	Curricular elements assigned to this level demand extended use of multiple higher-order thinking processes such as synthesis, reflection, assessment, and adjustment of plans over time. Students are engaged in conducting investigations to solve real-world problems with unpredictable outcomes. (Level 4 activities often require an extended period of time for carrying out multiple steps; however, time alone is not a distinguishing factor if the skills and concepts are simply repetitive over time.)	Make multiple strategic and procedural decisions when presented with new information throughout the course of the event. Engage in tasks that require perspective taking and collaboration with a group of individuals. Create graphs, tables, and charts to reason through and organize the information without instructor prompts.

Source: Adapted from Mississippi Department of Education, 2009.

In chapter 2, we discussed the process of unwrapping and how it assists teams as they clarify the standard's intent and identify its subset skills and concepts. As part of the process, teams can enhance their understanding of the end in mind by examining the DOK levels of each learning target.

Let's look at this example, in which a team examines the sixth-grade writing standard: "Write informative/explanatory texts to examine a topic and convey ideas, concepts, and information through the selection, organization, and analysis of relevant content" (W.6.2, NGA & CCSSO, 2010a). Through its unwrapping process, a sixth-grade English team identified the following learning targets and the DOK levels of each of those targets. See table 3.3.

Table 3.3: DOK Levels for Sixth-Grade English Learning Targets

Learning Targets	DOK Level
Know common informational text structures (for example, problem and solution, cause and effect, sequence).	DOK 1
Organize and analyze information from relevant sources.	DOK 2
Compose informative and explanatory texts that clearly convey ideas, concepts, and information about a chosen topic.	DOK 3

Figure 3.4 provides an alternative unwrapping template that assists teams in identifying their learning targets for a unit of study by level of rigor. Teams may also prefer to sequence their learning targets in the order that teachers will teach them in their instructional design. Please note that while there is no single right way to do this, it's critical that teams intentionally match the rigor of the learning target and the design of the assessment item or task.

Depth of Knowledge	Specific Learning Targets	Aligned Assessment Items
DOK 1 **Recall** What information, facts, simple procedures, properties, or definitions do we want students to know or recall?		

DOK 2 **Basic Reasoning** What basic reasoning and application of knowledge do we want students to demonstrate? May involve: • Compare and contrast • Classify • Convert information • Solve with formula		
DOK 3 **Strategic Thinking and Complex Reasoning** What higher-order, nonroutine, or complex thinking and analysis do we want students to execute? May involve: • Opinion or judgment • Critique		
DOK 4 **Extended Thinking** What complicated task or problem involving multiple higher-order thinking processes would students resolve? May involve: • Synthesis • Innovation • Reflection and adjustment to solve real-world problems		

Figure 3.4: Template for unwrapping based on level of rigor.

*Visit **go.SolutionTree.com/assessment** for a free reproducible version of this figure.*

By using the common language of DOK to describe the cognitive demands of learning targets, the team builds common clarity about the heart of the standard and what students will be able to demonstrate with appropriate instructional design. The team is now on the same page about the cognitive demand, which will help teachers develop both instruction and formative assessment items that match the demands and complexity of the learning targets.

Complexity of the Stimulus

Stimulus refers to the text, source, or graphical information the student receives as part of an assessment item. The stimulus provides information that students will use to answer the question. In assessment items targeting literacy, the stimulus may be a piece of text, which might be informational in nature, an excerpt from a literary piece or primary-source document, or text found in a more unconventional format, such as a table, chart, model, or illustration. It might even be a video or audio file.

In mathematics, the stimulus can be a particular problem type—perhaps real-world problems, charts, tables, graphs, or equations—that might contain unknown information. Within each of these categories, the construction or content of the stimulus can add to the rigor of the task based on many variables. While some assessment items may not require a stimulus, we urge teams to select them intentionally.

When we look at the major shifts in our more rigorous standards, we gain insight into how the stimuli we use in our assessments must also shift. Consider, for example, the priorities for literacy that have emerged with the CCSS. The standards are designed to ensure that students read increasingly complex texts closely, use evidence to justify their position or approach to a particular problem, and communicate and use their skills to dig deeply across content areas. Based on these priorities, we know that we need to ensure that our assessments use text of increasing complexity, ask students to support their reasoning using evidence, and spur them to apply these skills across content areas. Therefore, as we design quality assessments, we need to make certain that we hit the target when it comes to these areas. We've observed that text complexity is an area of particular challenge for teams.

In past efforts to categorize text, educators used word counts and readability scores, such as Lexiles (visit https://lexile.com for more about Lexiles). However, we know that text has many more dimensions to consider. Karin Hess and Sheena Hervey (2010) describe five practical parameters or elements to consider in addition to word length and Lexile levels when determining complexity of text: (1) format and layout, (2) purpose and meaning, (3) text structures and discourse, (4) language features, and (5) knowledge demands. We think these elements provide teams with a great framework for choosing text. Hess and Hervey's (2010) informational and literary text rubrics (provided in figures 3.5 and 3.6, pages 44–47) describe a progression of complexity within each of these elements and assist teams in selecting text ranging from simple to very complex. Using tools such as these empowers teams with the ability to be focused and intentional about their selection of text.

Tool 8	Gradients in Complexity:			
	Text-Complexity Rubric for Literary Texts			
Literary Text Analyzed (author, date):				
Overall Complexity Rating:			Notes:	
	Simple Text (1)	**Somewhat Complex Text (2)**	**Complex Text (3)**	**Very Complex Text (4)**
Format Layout	❑ Consistent placement of text, regular word and line spacing, often large plain font ❑ Numerous illustrations that directly support and help interpret the written text ❑ Supportive signposting (for example, chapter heading) and enhancements	❑ May have longer passages of uninterrupted text; often plain font ❑ A range of illustrations that support selected parts of the text ❑ Reduced signposting and enhancements	❑ Longer passages of uninterrupted text may include columns or other variations in layout; often smaller, more elaborate font ❑ A few illustrations that support the text or includes images that require some interpretation ❑ Minimal signposting or enhancements	❑ Very long passages of uninterrupted text that may include columns or other variations in layout; often small, densely packed print ❑ Minimal or no illustrations that support the text or includes images or text layout that require deeper interpretation (for example, symbolism or recursive reading) ❑ Integrated signposting conforming to literary devices; no enhancements

Purpose and Meaning	❏ Purpose usually stated explicitly in the title or in the beginning of the text (this is a story about . . .) ❏ One intended level of meaning or lesson ❏ Theme is obvious and revealed early in the text ❏ Common themes	❏ Purpose tends to be revealed early in the text, but may be conveyed with some subtlety ❏ More than one level of meaning, with levels clearly distinguished from each other ❏ Theme is clear and revealed early in the text, but may be conveyed with some subtlety ❏ More than one possible theme	❏ Purpose is implicit and may be revealed over the entirety of the text ❏ Several levels of meaning that may be difficult to identify or separate ❏ Themes may be implicit or subtle; are sometimes ambiguous and may be revealed over the entirety of the text ❏ Universal themes or archetypes (for example, the hero's journey)	❏ Purpose implicit or subtle; is sometimes ambiguous and revealed over the entirety of the text ❏ Several levels and competing elements of meaning that are difficult to identify or separate and interpret ❏ Themes implicit or subtle, often ambiguous, and revealed over the entirety of the text ❏ Universal themes or competing archetypes (for example, warrior versus hero)
Structure and Discourse	❏ Discourse style and organization of the text are clear, chronological, or easy to predict or follow ❏ Connections between events or ideas are explicit and clear ❏ One primary text structure is evident (for example, chronology)	❏ Organization of text may have two or more storylines or additional characters and is occasionally difficult to predict ❏ Connections among events or ideas are sometimes implicit or subtle ❏ Includes a main text structure with one to two embedded structures	❏ Organization of text may include subplots, time shifts, and more complex characters ❏ Connections among events or ideas are often implicit or subtle (for example, flashback establishes chronology) ❏ Includes different text types (diary entry or now a story within narrative) of varying complexity	❏ Organization of text is intricate with regard to elements (for example, narrative viewpoint, time shifts, multiple characters, storylines or subplots, detail) ❏ Connections among events or ideas are implicit or subtle throughout the text ❏ Includes sustained complex text types and hybrid or nonlinear texts (story within a story)
Language Features	❏ Mainly short, simple sentences ❏ Simple, literal language; predictable ❏ Vocabulary is mostly familiar for grade level; frequently appearing words	❏ Simple and composed sentences with some more complex constructions ❏ Mainly literal, common-use language ❏ Some unfamiliar or context-dependent, multiple-meaning, or precise words	❏ Many complex sentences with increased subordinate phrases and clauses ❏ Some figurative language or literary devices ❏ Includes much academic vocabulary and some domain-specific (content) vocabulary; precise language	❏ Many complex sentences, often containing nuanced details or concepts ❏ Much figurative language or use of literary devices (metaphor, analogy, connotative language, literary allusion, and so on) ❏ Includes extensive academic and domain-specific (content) vocabulary, and possibly archaic language

Figure 3.5: Text-complexity rubric for literary texts.

continued →

	Simple Text (1)	Somewhat Complex Text (2)	Complex Text (3)	Very Complex Text (4)
Background Knowledge Demands	❏ Minimal assumed personal experience or background knowledge needed ❏ Simple, straightforward ideas	❏ Some assumed personal experience or knowledge (for example, cultural or historical) ideas ❏ Both simple and more complex ideas	❏ Much assumed personal experience or explicit references to cultural, historical, literary, or political knowledge ❏ A range of recognizable ideas and challenging concepts or themes	❏ Extensive, demanding, assumed personal experience and implied cultural, historical, literary, or political knowledge ❏ Many new ideas, perspectives, or complex, challenging concepts

Source: Adapted from Hess & Hervey, 2010. Tools for Examining Text Complexity. *In Hess, K., 2013.* Linking Research With Practice. *www.karin-hess.com. Used with permission.*

Tool 7	Gradients in Complexity:
	Text-Complexity Rubric for Informational Texts

Informational Text Analyzed (author, date):		
Overall Complexity Rating:		Notes:

	Simple Text (1)	Somewhat Complex Text (2)	Complex Text (3)	Very Complex Text (4)
Format Layout	❏ Consistent placement of text; regular word and line spacing; often large, plain font ❏ Graphics, captioned photos, labeled diagrams that directly support and help interpret the written text ❏ Simple indexes; short glossaries ❏ Supportive signposting or enhancements	❏ May have longer passages of uninterrupted text; often plain font ❏ Graphs, photos, tables, charts, diagrams directly support the text ❏ Indexes, glossaries, occasional quotes, references ❏ Reduced signposting and enhancements	❏ Longer passages; uninterrupted text may include columns or other variations in layout; often smaller, more elaborate font ❏ Essential integrated graphics, tables, charts, formulas (necessary to make meaning of text) ❏ Embedded quotes, concluding appendices, indexes, glossaries, bibliography ❏ Minimal signposting or enhancements	❏ Very long passages; uninterrupted text that may include columns or other variations in layout; often small, densely packed print ❏ Extensive or complex, intricate, essential integrated tables, charts, formulas necessary to make connections or synthesize concepts presented ❏ Abstracts, footnotes, citations, or detailed indexes, appendices, bibliography ❏ Integrated signposting conforming to disciplinary formats; no enhancements
Purpose and Meaning	❏ A single or simple purpose conveying clear or factual information ❏ Meaning is clear; concrete with a narrow focus	❏ Purpose involves conveying a range of ideas with more detailed information or examples ❏ Meaning is more involved with a broader focus	❏ Purpose includes explaining or interpreting information, not just presenting it ❏ Meaning includes more complex concepts and a higher level of detail	❏ Purpose may include examining or evaluating complex, sometimes theoretical and contested information ❏ Meaning is intricate, with abstract theoretical elements

	Simple Text (1)	Somewhat Complex Text (2)	Complex Text (3)	Very Complex Text (4)
Structure and Discourse	❑ Discourse style and organization of the text are clear or chronological or easy to predict ❑ Connections between ideas, processes, or events are explicit and clear ❑ One primary text structure is evident (for example, sequence, description)	❑ Organization of the text may include a thesis or reasoned explanation in addition to facts ❑ Connections between some ideas, processes, or events are implicit or subtle ❑ Includes a main text structure with one to two embedded structures	❑ Organization of the text may contain multiple pathways, more than one thesis, or several genres ❑ Connections between an expanded range of ideas, processes, or events are deeper and often implicit or subtle ❑ Includes different text structure types of varying complexity	❑ Organization of the text is intricate or specialized for a particular discipline or genre ❑ Connections between an extensive range of ideas, processes, or events are deep, intricate, and often implicit or subtle ❑ Includes sustained, complex text structure types or specialized, hybrid text types, including digital texts
Language Features	❑ Mainly simple sentences ❑ Simple language style, sometimes with narrative elements ❑ Vocabulary is mostly familiar or defined in text	❑ Simple and composed sentences with some more complex constructions ❑ Increased objective style and passive constructions with higher factual content ❑ Includes some unfamiliar, context-dependent, or multiple-meaning words	❑ Many complex sentences with increased subordinate phrases and clauses or transition words ❑ Objective or passive style with higher conceptual content and increasing nominalization ❑ Includes much academic (nuanced) vocabulary or some domain-specific (content) vocabulary	❑ Mainly complex sentences, often containing multiple concepts ❑ Specialized disciplinary style with dense conceptual content and high nominalization ❑ Includes extensive academic (nuanced, precise) or domain-specific (content) vocabulary
Background Knowledge Demands	❑ General topic is familiar, with some details known by reader ❑ Simple, concrete ideas	❑ General topic is familiar, with some details new to reader (cultural, historical, literary, political, legal) ❑ Both simple and more complicated, abstract ideas	❑ General topic is somewhat familiar but with many details unknown to reader (cultural, historical, literary, political, legal) ❑ A range of recognizable ideas and challenging abstract concepts	❑ General topic is mostly unfamiliar with most details unknown to reader (cultural, historical, literary, political, legal) ❑ Many new ideas, perspectives, or complex, challenging, abstract, and theoretical concepts

Source: Adapted from Hess & Hervey, 2010. Tools for Examining Text Complexity. *In Hess, K., 2013.* Linking Research With Practice. *www.karin-hess.com. Used with permission.*

Figure 3.6: Text-complexity rubric for informational texts.

Align Assessment Items and Tasks With Rigor of the Learning Target

Whenever there is a disconnect between the learning target and the assessment question—that is, the question is either easier or more difficult than the learning target—the assessment is no longer valid. This disconnect frequently happens when the team fails to fully discuss the learning target's rigor during the unwrapping process or when the team chooses an assessment item from a text bank or textbook but doesn't carefully examine its rigor.

Ensuring that each learning target clearly connects to specific items or key features within assessment items is a key alignment strategy. Teams should reference the DOK levels when they design and align tasks that promote the complex thinking the standard targets. After members identify the DOK levels for each of the learning targets, they can brainstorm about the types of items they will design to more accurately measure each target. For example, let's examine how a team looks at a grade 5 standard and its major learning target:

> Determine a theme of a story, drama, or poem from details in the text, including how characters in a story or drama respond to challenges or how the speaker in a poem reflects upon a topic; summarize the text. (RL.5.2)

In table 3.4, the team identifies three major learning targets this standard comprises. They consider the DOK level for each learning target and design an assessment item that accurately measures the target with the intended rigor (see chapter 5 for a deeper discussion of types of assessment items, including selected and constructed responses).

Table 3.4: Aligning Learning Targets and Assessment Items With Rigor

Learning Target	DOK	Assessment Item
Determine the theme or themes of the text using details from the text to support their thinking.	Level 2	**Selected response plus highlighting:** After reading a brief passage, the student identifies the theme (for example, forgiveness, family, strength) and highlights supporting evidence.
Analyze how a character's response to challenges in a text impacts the theme of a story, drama, or poem.	Level 3	**Constructed response (using graphic organizer):** Using a map or graphic organizer to show cause and effect, student describes how a character responds to challenges and how that response impacts the theme of a story.
Write a summary using details from the text.	Level 3	**Constructed response (using a Google Doc):** Write a brief summary in response to the prompt.

Through this plan, teams can accurately assess each learning target using items that align with the level of rigor. They can assess them separately as formative measures, or clustered for a larger summative measure. Note that they also design the assessment items to gather evidence of student thinking in a reasonably efficient manner, and when teams examine the results, they will be able to draw a direct connection to the learning target. Chapter 4 continues the conversation about designing aligned assessment items.

Bring Students Into the Conversation

We can't emphasize enough the power of involving students in the assessment process. Doing so ensures that students are also empowered with knowledge about their targets for learning because they begin to own their learning and work in partnership with teachers to ensure they meet those targets with the desired level of rigor. Chapter 7 provides more detail about this concept, but for clarification, when we use the term *student-involved assessment*, it implies the following elements.

- **Students are absolutely clear on what they will learn and be able to demonstrate:** Marzano, Pickering, and Pollock (2001) establish that when students are clear on targets, they are more likely to hit them. In fact, it's common practice to ensure that students are clear on their learning targets using "I can" statements or similar approaches. We feel this is where the conversation around rigor begins. Not only do students need to understand the content of their targeted learning, but also how they will demonstrate the depth of their understanding. When presenting the learning targets, teams can structure their conversations to foster understanding about the larger purpose and application of those skills, including references to the thinking processes that students will use.

- **Students are clear on what quality looks like:** Using exemplary models of products that students will produce, teams can guide students to focus on key elements that reflect the level of depth and application they are targeting.

- **Students get regular feedback on their work:** Thinking critically and demonstrating higher levels of processing don't come naturally. Students need regular feedback on their work throughout the process. They also need guidance in how they use this feedback.

- **Students learn and use specific strategies to close the gap between their current performance and the targeted level of quality:** As active partners in their learning, students are empowered with a growth mindset and specific tactics designed to improve the accuracy and quality of their work.

One proven strategy to foster strong engagement and deeper understanding of the content is to have students construct their own questions to explore a topic (Rothstein & Santana, 2011). Another is to engage students in the design of a rubric with indicators that reflect critical thinking and inquiry. As part of the instructional design within a unit, teams can insert meaningful, scaffolded opportunities to intentionally engage students in the process of recognizing quality, getting and using feedback, and using that feedback to make adjustments to their work.

Conclusion

Across the years, the issue of rigor has infiltrated conversations related to standards, curriculum, and assessment. The standards now bring that topic to the forefront by intentionally defining rigor within the expectations for what students need to know and do. However, in order to ensure that all students receive the same high-quality instruction focused on that more rigorous end in mind, collaborative team members must recognize and clarify what that means for their instruction and assessments.

TIPS FOR TRACTION

- Be sure that your team discusses the end in mind considering the expected level of rigor. Use the common language of DOK to determine expectations for each learning target addressed in the unit.

- Remember that we define rigor by the tasks, assessments, or stimulus (such as the text) that we use to measure the attainment of the standards.

- Don't artificially bump up the rigor in a unit. Let the standards and their subset of learning targets dictate the rigor and create tasks accordingly. There will likely be an array of DOK levels in any unit of study.

CHAPTER 4

Intentionally Planning Instruction and Assessment

COMMON QUESTIONS AND CHALLENGES

- Do we all need to teach the same way? Do we have to teach the same thing on the same day?
- How do we find the time for corrective instruction or intervention?
- Must we use preassessment in our work?

In the last chapter, we looked at how changing standards have led to increased rigor of both instruction and assessment in our classrooms. Because most schools have changed both the standards and the high-stakes summative assessment used to measure student achievement, collaborative teams have been challenged to implement significant changes in their classrooms that go well beyond what might happen if a district were just writing a new curriculum or transitioning to a new textbook. In this chapter, we look at how high-performing teams align standards to both the instruction students receive and to the common formative and summative assessments teams use to monitor student learning along the way.

Once teams have identified essential standards and unwrapped them into learning targets, as we described in chapter 2, they can begin planning instructional units and common assessments—both formative and summative—based on these standards. They must determine units of study based on the essential standards, develop pacing guides that accommodate teaching, plan aligned instruction and assessments within curricular units, use preassessments when necessary, and ensure time for corrective instruction and intervention.

Identifying Units of Study

The first step in planning instruction is to determine what the units of study for the entire year or entire course will be, followed by assigning learning targets to those units. Be careful to assign all learning targets or standards to a unit—both the essential standards and the supporting standards (Ainsworth,

2010). We highly recommend highlighting the essential standards or targets in all curriculum documents and pacing calendars to remind teachers of the guaranteed curriculum.

As teams design units of instruction around these targets, they will notice that it's sometimes appropriate to place all of the learning targets from some standards in the same unit, and sometimes in different units. Consider the first-grade mathematics standard: "Add and subtract within 20, demonstrating fluency for addition and subtraction within 10" (1.OA.C.6, NGA & CCSSO, 2010b, p. 15). There are three explicit learning targets in this standard: (1) add within 20, (2) subtract within 20, and (3) demonstrate fluency for addition and subtraction within 10. Most first-grade teams would plan to spend time throughout the year on mastering these three targets and would not try to teach them all at the same time (within the same unit of instruction). On the other hand, consider the sixth-grade English language arts standard: "Trace and evaluate the argument and specific claims in a text, distinguishing claims that are supported by reasons and evidence from claims that are not" (RI.6.8, NGA & CCSSO, 2010a). There are also three explicit learning targets in this standard: (1) trace the argument and claims in a text, (2) evaluate the argument and claims in a text, and (3) distinguish claims that are supported by reasons and evidence from those that are not. Teachers are more likely in this case to teach all three of these targets together in the same unit.

As teams develop unit plans, it is important to make sure they use common formative assessments to identify which learning targets students continue to need help with. One of the most basic questions teams often ask us is, "How often is often enough to assess?" There are two things to consider when answering that question. The first is that teams new to this process need more time to write and use their assessments than teams who have more experience. The second is that teams must have time to respond to the resulting data during regular instructional time or the assessment will be worthless.

While there is no one right answer to this question, we believe it's important to know the research behind this issue. In a meta-analysis of research on the frequency of assessment, Robert L. Bangert-Drowns, James A. Kulik, and Chen-Lin C. Kulik (1991) conclude that the more frequently teachers use formative assessment, the greater the student achievement. We noticed that in this research the greatest gains came with at least one assessment every three weeks. After that, although the gains continue to grow, they grow at a slower rate. Thus, we advise collaborative teams to *start* with a goal of giving a common formative assessment every three weeks as they start this work. For teams who meet weekly, this time frame allows them one meeting to discuss the unit plan and essential standards, a second meeting to write the common formative assessment, and then the third meeting, which occurs after the assessment has been administered, for the team to examine its results and plan the corrective instruction. This becomes a recurring cycle of meetings the team follows throughout the year. In this same research study, Bangert-Drowns and colleagues (1991) found that although the greatest gains occurred using at least one assessment every three weeks, adding more frequent assessments continued to raise student achievement, albeit not at the same rate.

We've worked with some experienced teams who have almost weekly common formative assessments. One caveat applies for elementary teachers: because most elementary teachers teach all of the subject areas, we recommend that they decide whether to start with English language arts or mathematics first. Get comfortable with the process, from choosing essential standards to writing common formative assessments to using the data to know what to do next for students. For some teams, this will take a whole year. Others may feel comfortable adding the other subject after a semester. We recommend learning how to assess one subject well rather than trying to do both and not really learning from the process.

It is important, however, that *no* team takes a calendar and marks off three-week chunks to determine when it will assess. Instead, teams should examine when they teach their most essential learning targets in each unit. Plan a common formative assessment following this instruction. In units less than three weeks long, choose a time within that unit to use a common formative assessment to help structure the lessons toward the end of the unit.

As teams get more comfortable and confident in writing common formative assessments, they will find it easier to complete these tasks. We encourage teams to continue to add new common formative assessments around essential learning targets and to evaluate their effectiveness. We also recommend that teams consider whether they have a balanced assessment system in place. For example, if a school or district doesn't have either team-developed benchmarks, or those created by external test writers, it will be an important next step to create these assessments.

Developing Pacing Guides

A collaborative team might wonder what documents it needs to ensure the PLC process succeeds. Many schools and districts have done so with a variety of expectations about products, but we believe that all they need to have is a well-communicated set of essential standards and a pacing guide that ensures time for all teachers to effectively teach, assess, and provide corrective instruction. Teams must develop units of instruction that support the pacing guide and know specifically when they will teach and assess each of the essential standards or learning targets.

Once teams have assigned standards or learning targets to units of study, the next step is to develop a pacing guide for the year or course. The purpose of the pacing guide is to provide information about how much time teams will use to teach the assigned learning targets. We've seen pacing guides that range in specificity from describing which learning targets to teach on which date to just listing the units for each quarter of the school year and which standards to teach. We strongly recommend that teams not try to develop a daily pacing guide, as, in our experience, these rarely work as planned. Instead we suggest working either monthly or by grading period. Whichever choice the team makes, we recommend considering some additional ideas.

Teaching and Assessing Material

No one expects that every teacher on the team will teach the exact same thing on the same day. Schools should allow teachers to make decisions about how they want to teach the unit. One thing they will need to agree on, however, is when they will administer their common formative assessments. One question we often answer is whether all of the team members must give the common formative assessment on the same day. While no rule governs this, it is important that team members give the assessment in a timely manner so no teacher has to wait for his or her colleagues before responding. Consider the example of a four-member team that agrees to administer the common formative assessment any time during a particular week. If one teacher gives the assessment on Monday and another gives it on Friday, the team can't even meet to discuss how to respond until everyone has given it. This means that too much time will have passed for the students in the first class to receive corrective instruction. We've learned that it's best practice to agree on a specific date for the assessment, and then allow team members to determine how to get to that point using the instructional strategies they think are best. When the team builds consensus on this expectation, individual teachers will likely have to change some of their long-held practices.

However, the positive impact for students will be worth it. One of the benefits of common assessments is that they build in equity for students. There are no longer "easy" and "tough" teachers for a course or grade level. All teachers share the same expectations. We know, from experience, that the more that teams effectively use common formative assessments, the more they will agree about which strategies work best to teach specific skills and content. Pacing becomes less of an issue the longer teams work together.

Sometimes individual team members feel they have to vary the amount of time they need to teach certain concepts due to the diversity or makeup of their classes. Schools that operate as professional learning communities accept that all students must learn at high levels. They define *high levels* by agreeing to the essential standards for each grade or course. They don't back down on their rigorous expectations for their students based on who that student is or what his or her background might be. They do this by making sure that all students have access to the essential standards, spending more time on assessing and reteaching them, and placing less emphasis on the supporting standards. Differentiation also comes after the common formative assessment when a student might need extra time and support on an essential learning target or two. The students who have already mastered that target, as evidenced in the assessment results, receive an enrichment lesson related to the mastered target. We suggest that teams build a few flexible days into their pacing guides so that teachers are able to use their classroom formative assessments to determine whether the group needs additional time with a learning target.

Using Resources

One frequently asked question we hear is whether all teachers must use the same resources: pieces of texts or novels, manipulatives, websites, and so on. We believe that, if a teacher can ensure student mastery on the standards, the tools or resources used shouldn't matter. One caveat, however, is that departments often choose specific texts or novels to avoid asking students to read the same text in different courses or years. Therefore, having designated texts for courses becomes important. It's not uncommon for secondary departments to also decide on concepts, novels, or ideas that are important for all students. For example, a school might decide that all students should read at least one of Shakespeare's works. These decisions are important for any individual teacher to keep in mind when selecting materials.

Assessing Each Target

Another consideration in developing the pacing guide is how to determine when to assess each of the essential learning targets within the unit. Many teachers or curriculum writers like to use a spiral plan to teach certain learning targets—they teach them more than once and expect students to gather greater understanding each time. Collaborative teams need to review these targets and determine when to plan on assessing them for mastery. It's important not to wait until the end of the year to assess all of these targets because there won't be time to deliver corrective instruction and enrichment. Teachers might teach other essential learning targets one time and then assess them.

Accommodating Responsive Teaching

It is important that teams build time into the guide so that *every* time they give a common formative assessment, they have time set aside to respond to that information. Without it, or if they simply review the correct responses in class, they might as well not assess at all! How much response time is necessary varies depending on what the data provide, but we recommend planning for one class or lesson period per assessment.

Using Summative Assessments

While teams develop their pacing guides, they should also consider how (or if) they will use a common summative assessment. This assessment allows teachers—at the end of the learning or unit—to make sure that students can put all of the smaller learning targets together to answer broader questions. For example, in an essay-writing assignment, a teacher might formatively assess the opening paragraph, supporting details, and the word choice as students write but would consider the final essay product the summative assessment. In mathematics, one might use a summative assessment as a performance task that requires students to use a variety of learning targets to solve the problem.

Figure 4.1 shows what the pacing guide might look like after teams have considered these ideas. Visit **go.SolutionTree.com/assessment** for a free reproducible version of a blank pacing guide.

Essential Targets	Days Needed to Teach	Assessed on the Common Formative Assessment?	Assessed on the Common Summative Assessment?
Compare and contrast the overall structure of ideas, concepts, or information in two or more informational texts.	Three days	Yes	Yes
Quote accurately from the text when drawing inferences.	Two days	Yes	No
Write opinion pieces on topics or texts supporting a point of view with reasons and information.	Five days	Yes	Yes
Use context as a clue to the meaning of a word or phrase.	One day	Yes	No
Provide logically ordered reasons that are supported by facts and details.	Three days	Yes	Yes
Supporting Targets	Days Needed to Teach	Assessed on the Common Formative Assessment?	Assessed on the Common Summative Assessment?
In opinion writing, introduce a topic or text clearly; state an opinion.	Two days	No	Yes
In opinion writing, link opinions and reasons using words, phrases, and clauses.	Two days	No	No
In opinion writing, create an organizational structure in which ideas are logically grouped to support the writer's purpose.	Two days	No	Yes
Read with purpose and understanding.	Throughout the unit	Embedded in stimulus text	Embedded in stimulus text
Explain the relationship between two or more ideas or concepts in a scientific text.	Two days	No	No

Figure 4.1: Sample fifth-grade ELA unit pacing guide.

*Visit **go.SolutionTree.com/assessment** for a free reproducible version of this figure.*

If the pacing guide clearly shows which of the learning targets are essential and which are supporting, teachers can more easily commit to ensuring that *all* students have access to core curriculum. This is an important step in helping *all* students learn at high levels (Buffum, Mattos, & Weber, 2012).

Once teams begin to use a pacing guide, it becomes important to keep track of where the guide works effectively and where it doesn't. Some situations teams face affect the way they implement the curriculum. Consider how snow days, assemblies, field trips, and so on change the planned pacing. Teams must be flexible in their work so they are able to maneuver their instruction to ensure that students learn the essential standards. At the same time, teachers will find that their predictions about time requirements are not always accurate. Using summative assessments to evaluate the effectiveness of the pacing guide is an important step for teams as they reflect on their work. Visit www.kcsd96.org/curriculum /Elementary-Pacing-Guides.cfm for one exemplar of district-developed pacing guides from Kildeer Countryside Community Consolidated School District 96 (n.d.) in Buffalo Grove, Illinois.

Aligning Instruction and Assessment

Once teams have developed the pacing guide, it is time to design the lessons they will use in each unit. During this step, teams should examine each unit in more detail to highlight the essential learning targets they will assess on each common formative assessment. We recommend that they write the common summative assessment before teaching the unit, so that everyone on the team knows exactly what student proficiency on this topic will look like.

As we've said previously, it isn't important that all teachers teach the same thing on the same day. However, high-performing teams must consider how to ensure they are guiding students to the higher rigor the standards expect. "Learn together" has become a mantra of the teams we work with. High-performing teams study new research and new information in their content areas and around their grade levels. While it's important to avoid jumping from one new initiative to another, your team should stay abreast of what we know can help students achieve more. One of our favorite resources is *Visible Learning for Teachers* (Hattie, 2012). This compilation of research examines a whole host of innovations that researchers have studied and compares their effectiveness to each other.

Teams who learn together about the tasks associated with higher DOK levels and about how to scaffold ideas and strategies (as discussed in chapter 3) will more successfully meet these rigorous expectations. When they discuss this learning at their team meetings, they naturally become more cohesive in their pacing, and it supports their decisions about which instructional strategies work best. We also know that when these teams start examining the results of their common assessments, they naturally begin to see how some strategies work more effectively than others in helping students learn. This process is an important catalyst in building team consensus on pacing, instruction, and effective assessment.

The pacing guide might look something like the graphic in figure 4.2. Notice that the plan includes a day of response after every common formative assessment. While, in practice, this response may not happen on the day immediately following the common formative assessment, it must happen as soon as possible. The other thing to note is that this team has developed its unit plan based on a preassessment it's given. The team typically gives a preassessment a few days or even weeks before it starts the unit. This allows the team to consider the information from that assessment in its unit design.

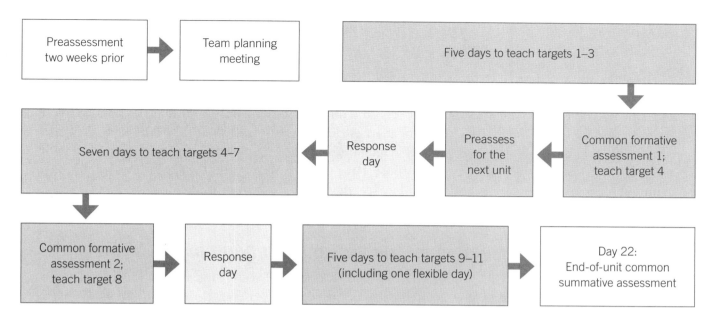

Figure 4.2: Developing a unit plan to include assessments.

These units of study identify for all teachers on the team the expected curriculum that they will use. As teams use summative assessments (common, benchmark, and end of year) they should examine the results to determine whether these units of study effectively ensure that students are reaching mastery on the correct curriculum. The units may need tweaks or even revisions to ensure alignment with the summative assessments.

Using Preassessments

While it might seem that we should address preassessment at the beginning of the chapter on developing units of instruction and pacing guides, we recommend that teams first make sure that they have created pacing guides that include all of the learning targets they are expected to teach during the school year. This is important because these guides are developed based on prerequisites students should already know from the pacing guides of the course or grade level prior to theirs. Then, the team may want to use preassessments with the students they are teaching during this school year.

Preassessment has two purposes, and how teams develop and use it is based on which purpose they establish. The first purpose is to determine what, if any, prerequisite skills students are missing. To gather this information, teams must plan the assessment around the essential prerequisite skills from prior years' content students must know to be successful in the upcoming unit. The second purpose is to establish what, if any, essential targets from the upcoming unit students have already mastered. In this case, the preassessment might either be, or resemble, the end-of-unit assessments that teams have planned for the unit they have yet to teach.

It is important for teams to establish ahead of developing the preassessment how they will use the information. When they use a preassessment to see if students lack prerequisite skills, identified students must receive intervention time to acquire these essential targets at a time where there is no new instruction occurring in the classroom, and before the beginning of the upcoming unit. When teams use a preassessment to see if some students have already mastered essential learning targets, the team will develop differentiated lessons that they can use with the identified students during the unit instruction.

In our work with teams, we have recognized that preassessments tend to be more difficult to write and use than common formative or summative assessments. Some teams try to develop both common assessments and preassessments simultaneously in a unit and often run into difficulties because their common formative assessments are different than preassessments—and should be different. They also confuse the two purposes of preassessments, which leads to creating preassessments that try to do both and really don't successfully fulfill either purpose. Because of this, we recommend that teams start with common formative assessments, and when they feel more confident with this work, they begin writing and using preassessments.

Accommodating Corrective Instruction and Intervention

We have never worked with a team who has told us teachers have *too* much time for this work! In fact, most teams feel they don't have enough collaborative time to get everything done and ensure their students master all that they teach. This is why consensus on the essential standards becomes such an important foundational piece to the assessment process. Teams guarantee these standards, and while they still teach the supporting standards, they have common agreement on what they will assess and reteach.

There are two types of response to assessments: (1) corrective instruction and (2) intervention. We use the term *corrective instruction* when we talk about how teams respond to the results of their common formative assessments in the regular classroom. All students receive this extra time and support during regular instruction; those who weren't proficient get more time and support on the essential learning targets they need help with, and students who were proficient extend their learning with additional work on these same essential standards. We distinguish this type of response from what we call *intervention*, a more intensive response that occurs *after* core curriculum and corrective instruction. Intervention happens during time teams have built in when no new instruction is taking place and when teams can flexibly group students based on their level of need. During this time, students who don't need intervention help may be engaged in enrichment activities or projects to help extend their learning. (See the section Responding Within the RTI Framework in chapter 6 for details on this process.)

In order to build in time to provide both levels of support, it is important that teachers agree to focus their core instruction and corrective interventions on the essential standards, recognizing that many students will learn much more than the essentials but *all* students must learn the essentials.

The next question about time that a school must address is how it will find time for Tier 2 and 3 interventions. While schools have found many creative ways to build in this time, there are a few specific ideas that many schools have used. For example, in elementary schools, the master schedule may be designed in a way that provides both common planning time for teachers to meet in their collaborative teams, as well as common teaching time when all students at a particular grade level are learning the same subject. The team can then designate an intervention block within this scheduled time where they will all be working on Tier 2 and 3 interventions for students who need more time and support as well as on enrichment opportunities for those students who are already proficient. Secondary schools may choose to build in one period several days a week or even every day, which is designated as intervention or enrichment time. Students may be assigned to homeroom, study hall, or advisory but can be assigned to a Tier 2 or 3 support group whenever needed. Thus, no one is pulled from one subject to get additional help for another subject. We highly recommend consulting *It's About Time: Planning Interventions and Extensions in Elementary School* (Buffum & Mattos, 2015) and *It's About Time: Planning Interventions and Extensions in Secondary School* (Mattos & Buffum, 2015) for other creative ways to make this work.

Conclusion

Once teams have planned instruction based on the essential standards, the best way to get started with assessment is to jump in and learn from mistakes as well as successes. Writing assessments and using assessment data are skills that teams develop over time. Each assessment teaches a team something new and helps it become stronger. We lay out the process to guide teams in creating assessment questions, tasks, and tools in chapter 5.

TIPS FOR TRACTION

- Use your essential standards as the focus of your common formative assessments. Don't try to assess everything—just the guaranteed and viable curriculum.

- Create a manageable pacing guide. Be attentive to when and where you teach and assess the essential standards. If you have curriculum material unrelated to the essential standards, it's time to get rid of it.

- Every time you plan a common formative assessment, make sure you build time into the regular instructional period to respond to the results.

- When developing a preassessment, be clear about its purpose. Is it to identify prerequisite skills students are missing, or is it to identify whether some students are already proficient on grade-level essential skills that you will teach?

CHAPTER 5

Creating Questions, Tasks, and Tools That Work

COMMON QUESTIONS AND CHALLENGES

- Are there some specific ways we can make sure our assessments produce the best information about what students need next?
- Do we need to worry about validity and reliability?
- How can we make sure students understand what we're asking them to do on an assessment?

We know how frustrating it can be for collaborative teams who are trying to analyze their assessment data to spend precious time examining the questions themselves to see if they misled students. When a significant number of students answer a question incorrectly, teachers wonder whether the question was confusing or the students simply did not master the learning target. If the questions are unclear or difficult to understand, teams worry that the assessment results won't really tell them what students still need to learn. In order for teams to ensure they design and write assessment items that will produce results they can count on, they must understand the various types of assessment items and the differences among them, develop strong rubrics based on these items, ensure valid data, choose the right stimuli, develop answer keys, and ensure assessment reliability and question quality.

Understanding Types of Assessment Items

Matching the essential learning target to the type of item helps increase the validity of the assessment. Consider teaching targets with high cognitive demand and then assessing only basic content. Students who do well on the assessment may not have really mastered the more rigorous content.

Let's start by exploring the most common types of items teachers use on their assessments: selected-response items, constructed-response items, performance items, and performance tasks. Each of these four types has both advantages and disadvantages, so it is important that teams choose which type they will use by looking at the proficiency expectations for the learning target. Teams can use multiple choice (selected response), for example, to assess vocabulary, content knowledge, and other lower-level learning targets, but those targets with high cognitive demand will likely require constructed response.

Selected-Response Items

Selected-response items provide answer choices, and the student must select the correct answer. Typically, these appear as multiple choice, matching, and true or false items. These items are easy to grade, don't require collaborative scoring to ensure team members all grade them the same way, often appear in high-stakes tests (making them good practice for students), and take a minimum amount of time to administer. However, they also allow students who don't know the answer to guess and are difficult to write at higher levels of cognitive demand.

Constructed-Response Items

Constructed-response items do not include the answer on the page; the student must supply it. Items that fit into this category are short- and extended-response questions, graphic organizers for students to complete (for example, a story map), and diagrams for students to fill in. These items can more easily assess higher cognitive demand, help teams understand students' misconceptions, and are often present on high-stakes tests. On the other hand, these items are more time consuming for students to take and for teachers to score, require collaborative scoring practice so that all teachers score them in the same way, and may be difficult for students who have trouble with writing.

Performance Items

Performance items ask students to demonstrate proficiency on a skill (for example, writing, playing an instrument, measuring, tumbling), and teachers typically score them with a rubric. They also include assessments that result in a product such as an essay, a drawing or painting, a piece of quality woodworking, and so on. These items are the best way to assess skills, are often engaging for students, reveal whether students can follow a step-by-step process, and may be based on realistic situations or activities. However, they also require a lot of student time to complete, a lot of teacher time to score, and collaborative scoring practices.

Teachers typically assess these items by observing the student do something, or by examining a final product. For example, consider this seventh-grade Speaking and Listening standard: "Come to discussions prepared, having read or researched material under study" (SL.7.1a, NGA & CCSSO, 2010a). The best way to assess this would be to observe students while they engage in a collaborative discussion. Other examples include a violin teacher who observes how a student holds a violin, an art teacher who provides feedback to a student about a drawing, or a speech teacher who monitors how well a student makes eye contact while giving a speech. You will notice that, in some of these examples, the teacher is going to either see the skill exhibited or not, and in other cases, the teacher will look for a proficiency range with a rubric.

Performance Tasks

Performance tasks have become more common as states using the CCSS often use these tasks on their end-of-the-year tests. Teams often develop similar tasks to use on their common formative assessments so students will have more experience with them as well as to be able to see if students can link several connected learning targets through planning and follow-through. SBAC (n.d.b) describes performance tasks as "collections of questions and activities that are coherently connected to a single theme or scenario." Teams design these tasks to be based on real-life or realistic situations; assess higher-cognitive-demand targets; require students to connect their ideas, plan problem solving, and follow a series of steps to get to the solution; and be more engaging than other items.

The student must typically navigate multiple stimuli, most often with multiple solutions and solution pathways. A performance task, therefore, represents a strong way to summatively assess students, revealing whether they can put together multiple learning targets to show what they know. Because teams build them around real-life situations, these assessments can motivate students. We suggest, as always, teams follow a protocol to develop strong tasks (SBAC, 2012c). See table 5.1 for an example.

Table 5.1: Protocol for Creating a Performance Task

Steps	Team Notes
1. Determine learning targets to include.	• It's important to integrate learning targets (for example, argument writing includes using research and supporting with evidence). • Look for targets with cognitive demand (requiring reasoning and thinking). • These targets may require students to research, plan, write, analyze, and justify. • As you get started, limit the number of learning targets until you and students are comfortable.
2. Create a realistic problem or scenario.	• Performance tasks should reflect a real-world task. • Students should be engaged and feel the task is worthwhile. • Tasks should allow for multiple points of view and have multiple correct responses. • Consider what the audience for the product will be.
3. Choose the stimulus.	• The stimulus or stimuli should be complex and meet the expectations for complexity of college and career readiness. • Providing too many unnecessary pieces of stimuli for the task may prevent some students from being able to reach proficiency.
4. Write the directions.	• Keep the directions as clear and as simple as possible. • Be very specific about any products or performances you expect students to produce.
5. Develop the rubric or scoring guide.	• Write the scoring guide so that students know exactly what they have to do to reach each level. • You may want to provide a checklist or a graphic organizer to help students know what they must provide in order to achieve a proficient or beyond proficient score.

Developing Strong Rubrics for Constructed Responses, Performance Items, and Performance Tasks

When teams create a constructed-response question, performance item, or performance task, they must also decide how they will score the item. It's important that all team members score the assessments in the same way. Because selected-response items are most often designed with one correct answer, there is no need to develop a rubric for these questions. We do, however, strongly encourage teams to develop an answer guide for all questions on each assessment to ensure that each team member is interpreting the question and answer the same way. If the common summative assessment the team develops has different weights for different items, it's important for the team to agree on how these items are weighted and

communicate that to students as well. For example, on an ELA summative assessment, the writing por-
tion may count as 40 percent of the score and the reading questions a total of 60 percent. By practicing
collaborative scoring on the constructed-response questions, performances, and performance tasks, teams
work together to ensure that no matter which team member scores an item, a student will receive the same
score. While there are many collaborative scoring protocols available (see reproducibles from *Collaborating
for Success With the Common Core* [Bailey et al., 2014] at **go.SolutionTree.com/commoncore**), they all
have the team select several pieces of student work, ask each team member to score them individually, and
then focus on building consensus on the final score.

When making scoring decisions, consider, first, whether the anticipated response will be definitive
(right or wrong) or whether there will be levels of proficiency. Some constructed-response questions have a
right or wrong answer. Consider, for example, these questions: What was the setting of the story? Which
data table supports the conclusions the author makes from the experiment? What can you infer about
the relationship between Sarah and her mom based on paragraph 16? While the student must supply an
answer to these questions, there is one correct answer. However, items with levels of proficiency require a
rubric for scoring. It's important that teams develop a student-friendly rubric for any constructed-response
items, performance items, or performance tasks so students understand what proficiency will look like.
When developing rubrics, teams should note the differences between analytic and holistic rubrics and
understand how to construct rubrics with strong criteria.

Analytic Versus Holistic Rubrics

Formative assessments need an *analytic rubric*. This type of rubric uses a separate set of criteria (row
on the rubric) for each learning target. This allows the team to respond to students' needs on a target-by-
target basis. For example, a student may be able to write a strong opening paragraph for his or her essay
but may not be able to provide details in subsequent paragraphs. By isolating each learning target for
feedback, teachers can provide the student with specific help.

A *holistic rubric* provides only one set of criteria for the entire student work. These are typically used
for summative assessments such as the PARCC or SBAC assessments. With this type of rubric, the student only knows the final score and may be less likely to learn from the feedback.

Strong Criteria in an Analytic Rubric

The first decision to make as a team when constructing rubrics is how many levels to use for the criteria. For standards-based grading, teams will likely use as many levels as are present on the report card.
A team might set up a typical rubric like figure 5.1.

Learning Target	Beyond Proficiency	Proficiency	Partial Proficiency	No Proficiency
Learning Target 1				
Learning Target 2				

Figure 5.1: Setting up a typical rubric.

In this case, the team will score two learning targets, and each target will have four levels of proficiency. For other assessments, the number of learning targets (rows on the rubric) will vary according to
what is being assessed.

In developing the levels of proficiency, teams typically start by clearly explaining what it will look like if the student is proficient on the learning target. Once they've described what proficiency will be, it's much easier to write the other levels: beyond proficiency, partial proficiency, and no proficiency. See figure 5.2.

Learning Target	Beyond Proficiency	Proficiency	Partial Proficiency	No Proficiency
Describe the information provided in both a firsthand account and a secondhand account.	Using a secondhand account of an event or topic, the student can rewrite it as a firsthand account showing how the information provided will change.	The student can list information provided from a firsthand and secondhand account and can summarize the differences.	The student can list details from each account but is unable to summarize them to show the connections.	The student is unable to list details about the information provided in each account.

Figure 5.2: A completed rubric for a learning target.

Not every learning target has a beyond level of proficiency. Consider the target: "Uses commas appropriately in writing." There is nothing students can show to demonstrate that they are beyond proficient. You'll notice in figure 5.2 that we've described a beyond proficiency level for the target that will likely require another item to be added to the assessment. In some cases the team offers this item for all students while they are taking the assessment (suggesting that they might want to try out this challenge); at other times the team may provide this question only to students who have demonstrated proficiency on the assessment. In fact, working on this challenge may be what students do during the corrective instruction time while the teacher is working with students who aren't yet proficient. In this case, the teacher gives the students a text that is written as a secondhand account and asks them to rewrite it as a firsthand account. This activity might be appropriate for students who were proficient during corrective instruction while the teachers work with students who weren't proficient.

Another piece of advice we offer is to make sure that rubrics reflect qualitative difference between the levels of proficiency. Consider the poorly written rubric in figure 5.3.

Learning Target	Beyond Proficiency	Proficiency	Partial Proficiency	No Proficiency
Explain how the main idea is supported by key details.	The student provides three key details.	The student provides two key details.	The student provides one key detail.	The student provides no key details.

Figure 5.3: A poorly written rubric.

You'll notice that in the rubric in figure 5.2, each level of proficiency was a qualitative difference between the level above and below. In this poorly written rubric, the team has used a quantitative difference for each level, which rewards persistence rather than greater understanding of the learning target.

Ensuring Validity

As collaborative teams develop assessments, whether summative or formative, they want to ensure that the items they write match the concepts that they guarantee students will learn. They want items to match both the content and the rigor of their essential learning targets. This results in *valid* data. There are two steps we recommend teams take to make their assessments valid. We described the first step, unwrapping the standards, in chapter 2. This process helps teams clarify what learning targets the students must learn to master a standard. As collaborative teams work on this process, they discuss the DOK level of the target and what it will look like for students to be proficient. As they begin to develop their assessments, the information they've learned from the unwrapping process helps them keep their items valid.

The second step in ensuring validity in teacher-written assessments is to create an assessment plan, prior to developing the actual assessment items, that determines what type of assessment items to use as well as how many items are necessary. We've used a template for our work on common formative assessments guided by an assessment planning protocol. See figure 5.4 for a blank template and table 5.2 for the guiding protocol.

Learning Targets	Level of Cognitive Demand				
	Recalling DOK 1	Basic Reasoning DOK 2	Strategic Thinking and Complex Reasoning DOK 3	Extended Thinking DOK 4	What Proficiency Will Look Like

Figure 5.4: Assessment planning chart.

*Visit **go.SolutionTree.com/assessment** for a free reproducible version of this figure.*

Table 5.2: Protocol for Assessment Planning

Steps	Team Notes
1. Determine which essential learning targets to include on the assessment and list them in the first column of the template.	Five minutes For a common formative assessment, there should be a maximum of three learning targets.
2. Review the DOK level associated with the learning target.	Three minutes
3. Decide what type of assessment item to use and how many will be necessary to ensure reliability. Match the rigor and type of learning target to the type of item that will best assess it.	Five minutes
4. Decide how many questions the student must get correct or what level of the rubric the student must achieve in order to be considered proficient, and list it in the final column under "What Proficiency Will Look Like."	Five minutes
5. Review the plan to consider how much time the assessment will take.	Five minutes

*Visit **go.SolutionTree.com/assessment** for a free reproducible version of this table.*

Notice that there are three empty rows in the template in figure 5.4 providing room for up to three learning targets in a common formative assessment. For each one, the teams agree on what the anticipated DOK level is for proficiency on that target. Using that information, they match the expected rigor to the type and number of items they will need to write. We've highlighted the DOK 3 and 4 columns to remind teams that using a multiple-choice item for these targets will likely not work.

One may wonder why we recommend that teams limit their common formative assessments to a *maximum* of three learning targets. We know that the more learning targets teams assess, the more time the assessment will take and the more complex the corrective instruction will be. For example, if a teacher assesses five learning targets, it's possible that a student could miss all five of them. Therefore, we recommend making assessments shorter and administering them more frequently. One of the implications of this advice is that even after a collaborative team has identified the essential standards, it will still be unable to assess all of the learning targets included in these standards due to the sheer quantity they will have on their list. We also have found in working with teams doing this work that they will be able to see that some targets from essential standards are more important than others. As teams plan their common formative assessments, we suggest looking for learning targets that come from essential standards and that also meet one of these three criteria.

1. Targets that are especially difficult or frequently lead to misconceptions

2. Targets that are prerequisite to future learning

3. Targets that are absolutely necessary for students to know

Note that when planning a common summative assessment that measures more learning targets, the team can simply add more rows to use the same planning template. Let's look at one example of how a team can ensure validity using the guidelines and tools we've provided here.

A fourth-grade team is working on a common formative assessment for the standard: "Interpret information presented visually, orally, or quantitatively (e.g., in charts, graphs, diagrams, time lines, animations, or interactive elements on Web pages) and explain how the information contributes to an understanding of the text in which it appears" (RI.4.7; NGA & CCSSO, 2010a). The team determines that for this common formative assessment it wants to assess the following targets.

- Interpret information presented quantitatively.
- Explain how the information contributes to an understanding of the text.

Based on these targets, the team develops an assessment plan using our assessment planning chart, as shown in figure 5.5 (page 68).

Note that in this example, the four multiple-choice questions will determine if the student has mastered the first learning target. The team agrees that students must get three of the four questions correct in order to demonstrate proficiency on this target. For the second learning target, the team creates the rubric in figure 5.6 (page 68) and agrees that students must reach proficiency to master this target.

Learning Targets	Level of Cognitive Demand				
	Recalling DOK 1	Basic Reasoning DOK 2	Strategic Thinking and Complex Reasoning DOK 3	Extended Thinking DOK 4	What Proficiency Will Look Like
Interpret information presented quantitatively.		Four multiple-choice questions			Three out of four correct
Explain how the information contributes to an understanding of the text.			One constructed-response question		Proficiency level on the rubric

Figure 5.5: Example of an assessment planning chart for grade 4.

One mistake we see some teams make is determining a *cut score* for the entire assessment. For example, the student must get 80 percent correct to be considered proficient. Can you see how this might allow a student to get two essential targets correct and one incorrect? If we agree that we are only assessing the *essential* learning targets, then we have agreed that the student must be proficient on them all. A student might be proficient on both learning targets, proficient on only target 1 or only target 2, or not proficient on either. How the team responds will be different based on each of these circumstances.

Learning Target	Beyond Proficiency	Proficiency	Partial Proficiency	No Proficiency
Explain how the information contributes to an understanding of the text.	There is no beyond proficiency level for this target.	The student is able to provide specific ways or examples of how the quantitative information supports the text or ways it doesn't support the text.	The student is able to explain how the quantitative information relates to the text, but is unable to determine if it supports it or not.	The student is unable to explain how the quantitative information relates to the text.

Figure 5.6: Example of a rubric for measuring a grade 4 learning target.

Choosing the Appropriate Stimulus

As we discussed in chapter 3, the stimulus a team chooses for its constructed-response items (or performance items and performance tasks) can increase the rigor of the item. SBAC has published a number of documents explaining its expectations for stimulus information in both mathematics and English language arts (SBAC, 2012a, 2012b, 2015a). While these documents cover the way that SBAC will choose the stimuli for its own end-of-year summative assessment, collaborative teams can learn some important information about how to choose the stimuli for their common formative assessments. For example, PARCC, SBAC, and many individual states have published expected Lexile ranges (a quantitative measure of text complexity) for text information. See tables 5.3–5.5 for information on Lexiles and appropriate text lengths for each grade level. Visit the Lexile website (http://lexile.com) to stay current with Lexile levels.

Table 5.3: Lexile Levels

Grade Band	Current Lexile Band	Stretch Lexile Band
K–1	N/A	N/A
2–3	450L–730L	420L–820L
4–5	640L–850L	740L–1010L
6–8	860L–1010L	925L–1185L
9–10	960L–1120L	1050L–1335L
11 through college and career ready	1070L–1220L	1185L–1385L

Source: Lexile Framework for Reading, 2016.

Table 5.4: Length of Text Per PARCC

Grade Band	Minimum and Maximum Length of Text
3–5	200–800 words
6–8	400–1,000 words
9–11	500–1,500 words

Source: PARCC, n.d.b.

Table 5.5: Length of Text Per SBAC

Grade	Word Count (Short Text)	Word Count (Long Text)
3	200–487	488–650
4–5	450–562	563–750
6–8	650–712	713–950
11	800–825	826–1,100

Source: SBAC, 2015a.

These guidelines should help teams decide whether a piece of text is appropriate to help students meet the expectations required of them. We know that if students always read less complex texts, they won't be proficient on the pieces of text in the end-of-the-year assessments. Additionally, as we discussed in chapter 3, text complexity is about more than a Lexile level. Both PARCC and SBAC have also published guidelines for the length of text they will use. As we work with teams, we've found this information helpful in determining how much text they should require their students to read to answer constructed-response questions.

Making sure the stimulus text supports the target or targets being assessed might be the hardest part of choosing one. For example, a team assessing how reasons and evidence support an argument must use a text written as an argument with some kind of support. In another example, a target might require two or more texts about the same topic. As the CCSS have become more mainstream, we've noticed that these types of texts are becoming much easier to find. Many online resources are available and easy to access, including: Newsela (https://newsela.com), ReadWorks (www.readworks.org), EDSITEment! (https://edsitement.neh.gov), and The Learning Network (learning.blogs.nytimes.com) to name a few. We still encourage teams to be very selective about the texts they choose.

The same is true for stimuli from other subject areas, such as realistic or real-life problems in mathematics, data tables and graphs in mathematics, primary-source documents in social studies, and experimental designs in science. The stimulus must match the rigor and content of the learning target.

Developing the Answer Key

Another common mistake we've seen in data meetings is when teams fail to agree on correct answers prior to giving the assessment. When they get together to talk about what to do next for students, they have to back up and talk about what answers are acceptable. Establishing upfront what correct or proficient answers look like is especially important with constructed-response questions, as there are typically multiple ways a student can correctly answer the question. The answer key must also include information about which questions address which learning targets and how many questions the students must get correct to be proficient. We recommend that teams always create the answer key as they write the questions. In addition to listing correct answers, some teams find it helpful to anticipate the incorrect answers they think students might use.

Continuing the fourth-grade example, the team finds a science article about global warming that includes a data table with information about temperature over time, the sea level, and the amount of land ice. As the team works on the questions it will ask, members agree on what the correct and incorrect answers will be for this target using this text. The multiple-choice questions are easy to include in their answer key, but the constructed-response question requires them to think about what students will need to include, what it might look like if they are partially proficient (what they will likely miss), and what an answer that isn't proficient looks like.

Ensuring Reliability

We consider an assessment reliable when teachers feel confident that the information they are getting really does identify which students have reached proficiency and which have not yet reached it. For teacher-created assessments, this means there are enough items that teachers can rule out lucky guessing as a way to appear proficient, as well as tricky or vague questions as a way to make proficient students appear as if they don't know the learning targets. We are comforted by Douglas Reeves (2007), who reminds us of the importance of choosing practicality over psychometric perfection—that is, that teachers don't have to field test questions or apply statistical analysis because the results are being used to guide instruction rather than make high-stakes decisions about whether a student is admitted to college or given college credit on an AP exam. However, we still know that teachers want to make their assessments as reliable as possible so they aren't wasting important instructional time administering and responding to them.

We recommend two ways to make assessments reliable. The first is to make sure to include enough questions for each of the assessed learning targets. While there is no one piece of research that supplies the answer to how many questions this would be, most researchers suggest that at least three to four selected-response questions per learning target will eliminate lucky guessing (Gareis & Grant, 2008). For constructed-response questions, one well-written question should instill confidence in a team that it can decide on next steps for the student.

The second strategy for making team-designed assessments reliable is to make sure each question itself is clear and understandable to students. Consider Stephen Chappuis, Jan Chappuis, and Rick Stiggins's (2009) advice: write the question itself at the lowest possible reading level. This recommendation is important to eliminate student misunderstanding regarding what the question is asking. Please note that this advice does *not* refer to the stimulus text the students might have to read prior to answering the question. We sometimes see items that confuse students because of their structure, or because they include negative terms that will throw off some students who actually know the content of the question. Therefore, we feel it's important for teams to learn how to write questions that will lead to better student responses. For example, the question "Which of the following sentences is not an example of correct grammar?" might be more difficult for students to answer than asking the reverse: "Which of the following sentences uses correct grammar?" Also, the question "Tell me what you've learned about fireworks after reading this text?" is too vague. Consider instead "After reading this text about fireworks, list three scientific concepts that the author explained in it."

Ensuring Quality of Questions

In our work with teams as they begin writing assessments, we've found that often they believe that they don't have the knowledge they need to develop good questions and quality assessment items. However, we know the opposite is true. Collaborative teams who have been determining essential standards, unwrapping them, and developing pacing guides and associated instructional practices are far more informed about how best to assess than anyone else. However, we also know that there will be times after teachers give an assessment when a question that seemed clear to the team might not be as clear to the students. When this happens, remember that the team *owns* this assessment. That means the team decides whether to simply eliminate the results from this question when developing corrective instruction or give a rewritten question before starting it. Either way, it's important to keep good records to avoid using the same unclear question again next year.

Figure 5.7 provides a quick tool that teams can reference when asking the question "Are our assessments designed well?" We call it the ACID (aligned, clearly written, informative, designed) test—a set of questions that prompt teams to consider and quickly review their products. The tool also offers team strategies that will assist in the design of quality common assessments. Visit **go.SolutionTree.com/assessment** for an additional "Writing Quality Questions" reproducible containing reminders that teams can refer to for developing quality questions during their meetings while they are writing assessment items.

A	Is the assessment *aligned* to the context, content, and rigor or complexity of the standards?
	• Look at the language of the standard and the learning targets (from the unwrapped standard) in comparison to the task. Are the thinking types on the assessment aligned to those targets?
	• Do the various items target the various levels of rigor or application (for example, DOK) represented in the learning targets? For example, is the difficulty of the task or questions at the same level as the target?
	• Examine any exemplars related to your targeted level of complexity. Is the level of scaffolding or cueing appropriate?
	• Is the designated level of mastery or proficiency appropriate and aligned?

Figure 5.7: ACID test.

continued →

C	Are the items on the assessment **clearly written**?
	• Read the prompt and any distractors provided. By completing this task as written, will students be demonstrating the skills and concepts you are targeting?
	• Will students understand what you want them to do?
I	Will this assessment be **informative** about student learning and produce meaningful data?
	• Will teams benefit from gathering data on these learning targets in this fashion?
	• Will specific information on learning targets steer teams toward meaningful interventions and support?
	• Will this assessment be an opportunity to provide feedback to students?
D	Is the assessment **designed** to reflect and support the demands of the standards?
	• Will the items ask students to show what they know in a way similar to high-stakes assessments?
	• Are students asked to provide reasoning for their answers?
	• Are students looking for evidence?
	• Are students digging into information in a variety of texts and sources?

*Visit **go.SolutionTree.com/assessment** for a free reproducible version of this figure.*

The following subsections provide specific information about ensuring quality in (1) constructed-response questions and (2) selected-response questions.

Constructed-Response Questions

Because so many of the high-stakes tests now use some version of constructed-response questions, and because these items reveal so much more about student learning than selected-response questions, it is important that teams ensure the quality of their constructed-response questions. Here, we explore two ways teams can design quality questions: (1) provide context and (2) be explicit about expectations.

Provide Context

In writing a quality constructed-response item, teams need to provide context that will help students connect with what the assessment is asking them to do. One way is to link the question to a learning target they have been working on in class. For example, when a mathematics question includes the phrase "use the ideas of center and spread," the students know that they are to solve a task using central tendency. This doesn't give away the answer but helps the student see the context of the question. Or consider another example: "In class we studied how an author uses rhetoric to convince a reader of something. Explain how the author of this text uses rhetoric to convince the reader to support his immigration policy." The students can then connect specific ideas they have studied about rhetoric to a new situation.

Another way to add context to an item is to narrow its focus. Consider this sample item: "After analyzing the primary-source documents provided, consider what information Truman had about the consequences of the atomic bomb when he chose to use it on Japan?" In this case, students don't supply their own knowledge, but rather use information from the documents provided.

Finally, the context might ask students to connect ideas in a different way. Consider this sample constructed-response item: "In class we studied how a cell membrane is selectively permeable. Consider what would happen if a cell's membrane was *not* selectively permeable. Provide at least two cell functions that would change as a result and explain what effect this would have on the cell." This twist on the learning target requires the students to do more than just repeat information they learned during class discussion. They must show understanding of the concept and how it might apply in a different situation. The context of the item should help students better understand what it asks them to do.

Be Explicit About Expectations

Explicitness about expectations for students' answers helps ensure teams create quality constructed-response questions. Teams should make sure students know how many examples to provide in their responses, or what information they need to provide in addition to the right answer. Do they have to show their work in mathematics? Justify their answer with textual evidence? Provide *three* examples? We've found that supplying a graphic organizer with the question helps students provide all the evidence the question asks for and, at the same time, makes their responses easier to score. Consider the organizer in figure 5.8 for a question that asks for three examples from the text and a citation for each one.

Example From Text	Citation
1.	
2.	
3.	

Figure 5.8: Graphic organizer for answering a constructed-response question.

Selected-Response Questions

Assessment researchers (Gareis & Grant, 2008; Popham, 2003; Stiggins, Arter, Chappuis, & Chappuis, 2004) have written much more about creating quality selected-response questions than about creating quality constructed-response questions. The most common selected-response item is some version of a multiple-choice question. Here, we share some of the important points research has yielded about how to create quality multiple-choice questions.

Multiple-choice questions comprise two parts: (1) the item stem and (2) the answer choices. The item stem is the statement or question that precedes the answer choices. Teams should write good item stems as complete sentences or questions that require students to read all the way through it before considering the answer choices (Gareis & Grant, 2008; Popham, 2003; Stiggins et al., 2004). Be careful not to provide clues about the correct answer by pairing a singular verb with answers that would require a plural verb (for example, consider the question "Who is the main character in the story?" and then having one of the answer choices as Sarah and Sam. Students can eliminate this as the correct answer because the stem is written to include a single person as the correct answer) or using the article *an* when the choices include answers that start with a consonant. As previously noted, we discourage negative language in the stem, such as, "Which of these is *not* an example of a democracy?" While we know that many high-stakes tests include these types of multiple-choice questions, we also know that this can confuse students who actually know the learning target (Gareis & Grant, 2008; Popham, 2003; Stiggins et al., 2004). We recommend providing opportunities to practice these types of questions when teaching students test-taking techniques. This makes more sense than using them on actual common formative assessments. One final suggestion for item stems is to be very clear when asking for the *most likely* or *best* answer by using boldface or italicized print (Gareis & Grant, 2008). For example, "Which of the choices represents the *best* solution to Jeremy's problem with the lost dog?"

The other part of a multiple-choice question is the answer choices. Traditionally, multiple-choice items have one correct answer. However, within state- and benchmark-level assessments, we have seen an increase in items that require students to choose *all that apply* or similar responses. Regardless of a requirement to select one or more correct responses, the other choices are called the *distractors*. When developing distractors, we recommend that teams consider typical mistakes students make or misconceptions they may have about the learning target they are assessing. This makes teams better able to analyze errors to determine how best to respond to students who still need help on the learning target. We explore this process in more detail in chapter 6.

It's important that all answer choices are reasonable. When students see choices that are funny or not possible, they start to look for other questions with similar answer choices and can lose concentration on the purpose of the assessment. Use answer choices with parallel grammatical structure and of similar length. Consider the multiple-choice question "Why would parents seek the counsel of a genetic counselor?" followed by the answer choices: (a) to know what their child will look like, (b) they want to pick the sex of their child, (c) there are some inherited disorders that they want to make sure their child doesn't have, or (d) to find out the hair color of the baby. Students who've studied test-taking strategies know that if an answer is much longer than the other answers, it's likely the correct answer and can more easily guess correctly even if they don't know the learning target. So, instead, better answer choices might be: (a) to find out what their child will look like, (b) to find out the sex of their child, (c) to find out if their child might have an inherited disorder, or (d) to find out the hair color of their baby.

Be careful not to overuse *all of the above* and *none of the above*. Sometimes teams add these choices to achieve an equal number of answer choices for each question. Researchers suggest that there is no one best answer to the question "How many answer choices should I use?" but indicate that three choices can be effective if they are well written (Haladyna & Downing, 1989; Rodriguez, 2005).

Put answer choices in a logical order—alphabetical, numerical, or chronological. We know that if teams aren't purposeful about this order, they often resort to making *c*, *d*, or *e* the default choice (Popham, 2003). They do this because they want students to have to read all the answer choices. Students who don't know the answer can then guess and be more likely to appear to know the target (Gareis & Grant, 2008; Popham, 2003; Stiggins et al., 2004).

Finally, make sure that the correct answer is the *only* correct answer. Teams sometimes teach a target a particular way and don't see that they have included another correct answer among their choices.

Putting It Into Practice

The following scenario illustrates the process a team might go through as it creates quality assessments. Five members of a fourth-grade team meet to plan an upcoming common formative assessment. Jason Baker, who is the team leader, quickly reviews the norms so the team can accomplish this task in the forty-five-minute planning period it has today. As the team members start planning the assessment, he asks them to review the essential learning targets they've been working on to determine which they will assess. They decide they want to use a piece of informational text for this assessment and review the following essential learning targets specifically related to informational text for this unit:

Describe the overall structure (e.g., chronology, comparison, cause/effect, problem/solution) of events, ideas, concepts, or information in a text or part of a text. (RI.4.5)

Use context (e.g., definitions, examples, or restatements in text) as a clue to the meaning of a word or phrase. (L.4.4a)

Refer to details and examples in a text when explaining what the text says explicitly and when drawing inferences from the text. (RI.4.1)

When this team begins the planning and writing process, it uses a Google Doc projected on a screen so everyone can see the product it develops. Andrea Carlson is the team record keeper. She pulls up a blank planning template and asks the team members whether they want to assess all three targets or narrow their focus. Jason suggests that they should definitely include the vocabulary target, as this has been a major focus of their time, and also advises that they include the text structure target because they already taught it in the last unit but did not assess it. Andrea suggests that they limit this assessment to these two targets, both because they want to keep the assessment short and they also regularly assess the third target on several other assessments. The team agrees to assess the first two targets. The members quickly review the DOK levels they assigned to these two targets when they unwrapped the standards to make sure they are in agreement before they write their assessment. They assign both of these targets a DOK level 2.

Jason then asks the team members whether they have an idea of a piece of stimulus text. No one has a piece of text in mind, so the team members begin their search. Sean Miller likes the *National Geographic* website and suggests they start there. When they pull up this website and search for an article to use, they find one about an accident on Mount Rainier. As they review the article, they don't feel it's a strong match for what they want, but Sean remembers a piece of text about volcanoes listed in appendix B of the Common Core State Standards (NGA & CCSSO, n.d.b). They pull up that document and find the source is a book called *Volcanoes* by Seymour Simon (1988). As they read the excerpt, they decide it's a great match: the vocabulary is defined in several different ways, and it includes a definition of some words that appear at the end of the sentence:

Our planet is made up of many layers of rock. The top layers of solid rock are called the crust. Deep beneath the crust is the mantle, where it is so hot that some rock melts. The melted, or molten, rock is called magma. (Simon, 1988, p. 6)

This requires students to use several different context clues that teachers gave them in this unit. The excerpt contains a compare-and-contrast section about two different volcanoes—Mount Rainier and Mount Adams—that work well with that learning target. The team plans to use pages 6–9 from the text for the stimulus.

Andrea begins to complete the assessment plan listing the two learning targets. Since both of the targets are DOK level 2, they know that they can choose to use either multiple-choice or constructed-response questions. Mary Sherman recommends they use a constructed-response question for the text structure target that will ask the students to explain not only why they believe the structure is compare and contrast but also ask the students to share details from the text to illustrate why they determined this to be so. Jason suggests that they use three multiple-choice questions to assess the vocabulary target since this is what the end-of-year test will ask students to do.

Evaluating for Continual Improvement

Just as we've discussed in previous chapters, it's important that teams take time after each assessment to reflect on the assessment itself. Once a team has used an assessment, it's always good practice to look at how effective the student answers were to determine who needs extra time and support and what kinds of support that should be, as well as who can benefit from enrichment on these learning targets. The team should reflect on the assessment plan as well as the questions, anticipated answers, and rubrics. This reflection can take place during the same meeting in which team members analyze data and plan corrective instruction. Whether the team wants to use the assessment again next year, or whether it wants to learn from its own work, taking a few minutes to ask, "Did this assessment work the way we wanted it to?" is worthwhile. When teams have ideas for improvement, they should make sure to put them in writing so they can apply them in the future.

Conclusion

The discussions in this book might make it appear that all of the teams we've worked with have plenty of team time to collaborate and plenty of instructional time to respond to student needs. However, in reality this is not the case. We advise the teams we work with to think big and start small. If a team understands the big picture of assessment and how common assessments fit in, that's a great starting point. Pick one learning target from an upcoming unit that everyone can agree is essential. Write a short common formative assessment that meets the rigor of that target and examine the resulting student work. Teams may be surprised at the results. We remember one middle school social studies teacher who said to her colleagues after their first common formative assessment, "I can't believe how much I learned about what the students knew and didn't know from one constructed-response question!" She likely had used constructed-response questions in her work before, but probably had only thought of the student responses in terms of how many points they warranted. Just changing the perspective to the question, What does this response tell me about what this student understands?, makes a huge difference in how teams use assessments. Remember, although this work is complex, if teams start small, the path gets clearer as they move forward.

In chapter 6, we discuss how teams use the results of their common assessments. When teams use the assessment planning process and write quality questions, the next step is an easy one.

TIPS FOR TRACTION

- Short, frequent common formative assessments allow you to respond quickly to the most important learning targets.
- Planning your assessment prior to writing the questions allows you to create a more valid assessment. You know you'll get back the right information when you plan first.
- When you use constructed-response questions, you learn not just which students need additional help but what students' misunderstandings and misconceptions are.
- Create the answer key as you develop the assessment items. This ensures your team has a common agreement about the correct answer.

CHAPTER 6

Using Data to Support Student Learning

COMMON QUESTIONS AND CHALLENGES

- Why do we need formative assessments if we already know which students have failed to master an essential learning target?
- Is there a difference between how we use summative data and formative data?
- How do we know what kinds of responses are most effective when looking at data?

While states adopt more rigorous standards, one thing hasn't changed: the overwhelming amount of data available for teachers and teams to use to guide their work. We rarely hear teachers complain that they don't have enough data about their students. However, we do encounter many teams that don't believe they have the right data to meet their needs. Most educators understand the power associated with using formative assessment. Unfortunately this emphasis on formative assessments has led some teachers to overlook the importance of summative assessments.

We've also heard lots of teachers, administrators, consultants, and authors spend a great deal of time debating the differences between formative and summative assessment. Sometimes in workshops, people will ask us, "If I'm using the results from our state test to identify students who need intensive support, doesn't that make the state test formative?" This question led us to realize that distinguishing between formative and summative *had* to be more than just a vocabulary debate. Rather, the question teams should be considering is how they are going to use the data to determine which type of assessment they want to create and how to best design that assessment. If they want to be able to diagnose students' needs and plan how to respond to these needs, the team needs to design their formative assessment around learning targets. If the team wants to make decisions about student growth, determine how effective their action plan is for their SMART goals, or critique their instructional practices or pacing guides, they need a summative assessment written around the standards. We know that we must have data from both formative and summative assessments to guide our work, but teams need to be clear about which types of data will provide the best information for their different purposes.

In chapter 1, we explored the various types of assessments teams should use to guide their instructional decisions, as well as the purposes of those assessments. In this chapter, we look more specifically at how a team uses the data from these assessments to make accurate decisions about what to do next for their students.

Establishing Trust

Before teams can constructively analyze data, they must ensure a certain level of trust among their members. Without trust, sharing beliefs about assessment and priorities, and especially sharing data, can threaten teachers. Therefore, it's very important for teams to make sure they have strong norms in place before they begin analyzing and responding to data. In fact, we recommend that teams consider whether they have *data norms* to guide their work. These govern how team members behave when they work with data. Some suggestions include the following.

- We will not compare scores with the intention of judging each other.

- We will use data to help each other and our team get better at what we're doing.

- We will use data for what they tell us to do next, and will not make excuses about them.

Having such norms in place helps create a more comfortable, safe, and trusting atmosphere for teams and allows them to be more honest in their work together and achieve better outcomes.

Ensuring Actionable Data

Data-driven schools and teams have identified the purpose of the data they are using and ensured that the data will be actionable. *Actionable data* means that the information allows team members to respond in a way that will increase student learning. It's important that when examining these data, a team looks not only at scores and percentages but also at the student work itself. If the value of common formative assessments is that we uncover student thinking, and especially their misconceptions, we need to have actual student work at the table during our data analysis process. This allows us to develop different responses depending on the student misunderstanding or misconception.

There are really two levels of action that teams take with their data, and they relate to the two types of questions we introduced in chapter 1: wide-angle questions and close-up questions. When asking wide-angle questions, teams set a SMART goal (a goal that is strategic and specific, measurable, attainable, results oriented, and time bound; Conzemius & O'Neill, 2014) for student learning and monitor whether their action plan is effective in achieving it. The team relies on more summative data to set and monitor goals. Team members develop these assessments around a larger grain size (typically a standard) and intend them to help chart student learning over time. The term *grain size* when applied to assessment refers to the size of the information being reported, and the grain size of the assessment items must match the kind of information we need to get back (Popham, 2007). To diagnose specific student needs, we want to be able to get information back in a small grain size, therefore, we write questions about learning targets rather than standards. If we are critiquing our team practices, we need a larger grain size and often want the information back based on standards. By asking close-up questions, teams use common formative assessments, which provide specific information to determine what to do next for students experiencing difficulty in learning. With common formative assessments, we know that the grain size should be smaller and based on learning targets, which allow teams to diagnose exactly how much additional time and support students need.

Teams should be aware of how balanced their own assessment system is with regard to types and amounts of actionable data sources. They should not only make sure they are using the right data for the right purpose but also determine whether they have available assessments (or are working to develop them) for each purpose. They also should be aware of situations where they may be using redundant assessments for the same purpose. For example, we've worked with teams who have a wide variety of summative assessments (end of unit, midterm, benchmark, final, end of year) but have few formative assessments. In such cases, teams may want to eliminate some of the assessments they do have to make additional time for the assessments they want to add.

Understanding and Using Common Summative Data

In chapter 1, we identified different ways that teams access summative data: classroom unit tests, common summative assessments, benchmark data, and state test data. Each of these data sources provides a measure of student learning; they tell us whether the student is below proficiency, at proficiency, or beyond proficiency. Sometimes we express this measure as a percentage (unit test), scaled score (a score from a standardized test that allows us to compare one test's results to another), or even RIT (Rasch Unit) score (a score used on a standardized test that allows reporting of student growth). One common misconception (often encouraged by vendors who want to market their products) is that summative data can show how to support students during interventions. Salespeople from assessment companies will try to convince teachers that their "Common Core–aligned, high-stakes predictors" can identify students in need, show what to teach them next, and monitor their progress on *everything*; however, the reality is that summative data can't accomplish these things. Summative data usually just aren't specific enough to do this effectively; formative data help us here. In addition, unless the district or teacher teams develop them, summative assessments do not tightly align to the curriculum in the classroom. Consider the fact that a teacher might finish teaching equivalent fractions in his or her classroom and might provide some fraction problems on the summative assessment, but that's where the alignment ends. In addition, summative assessments typically happen at the end of the learning process, rarely in time to inform decisions before teams are ready to start a new unit of instruction. We often see teams make the same mistakes we made early in our own learning about assessment—we highlighted the data, graphed the data, disaggregated the data, and reaggregated them. We thought that if we had a better way to analyze these data, we could make them meaningful. What we finally realized was that we were working with the wrong data and that they wouldn't tell us what to do next for our students no matter how we analyzed them.

Instead, summative assessments tell us whether students can integrate several learning targets to develop a full understanding of the standards; they measure student learning against the established standards we want them to learn. We use this type of data for a variety of purposes; some are student related but others relate to curriculum, pacing, and instructional decisions. Student-related purposes include identifying students who need urgent support, prerequisite skills and concepts that students are missing, and students' strengths and weaknesses. Other purposes include setting and monitoring team SMART goals, examining the effectiveness of our instructional strategies and curriculum, evaluating our pacing guides, and providing feedback on whether we've chosen our essential standards well.

When a collaborative team analyzes this type of data, we recommend members use a different protocol than when they examine common formative data. In each case, using a protocol to guide data discussions helps keep the team on topic and on time. Without a protocol, teams tend to move in many different directions and aren't always able to use their collaboration time effectively. A protocol also helps teams navigate discussions that might be uncomfortable, such as when teachers are comparing results with each other. Consider the protocol we have developed for using common summative assessment data in table 6.1.

Understanding and Using Common Formative Data

We have heard many collaborative teams comment that they already know which of their students will pass or fail a formative assessment before they give it. They remark that they have worked closely with their students during the instructional process and often ask why they still need to use common formative assessments in their work.

The answer to this question became clearer to us when we worked with one second-grade team. The teachers had selected the following Reading Standard for Informational Text as an essential standard for their second graders: "Identify the main topic of a multiparagraph text as well as the focus of specific paragraphs within the text" (RI.2.2). The team found a two-paragraph informational text for students to read and then asked them two questions: "What is the main topic of this text?" and "What is the focus of paragraph 1 and for paragraph 2?" During our visit, the teachers brought their student work to the table and began their data discussion by making two piles based on the first question. One pile represented the students who answered the question correctly and the second those who answered it incorrectly. As they finished, one teacher observed that almost all of her students who had answered the first question incorrectly had written the first sentence of the first paragraph. The other teachers concurred and started to talk about why the students would think this was the main topic. One thing that came up in this conversation was how they taught paragraph writing—they instructed students to start with the topic sentence and then add details. They realized that they had led students to believe that the topic sentence was always the first sentence of the paragraph. Two strategies emerged from this conversation. The first was that they would address this misconception in their corrective instruction by having students look at several different pieces of text with at least one where the main topic wasn't the first sentence. The second strategy was to make sure that when they taught paragraph writing to show students how the topic sentence could be somewhere else in the paragraph rather than the first sentence.

This conversation made the definition of formative assessment much clearer for this team. They realized that, more than just a way to identify which students have mastered the learning targets and which students have not yet mastered them, a formative assessment should expose the students' thinking in a way that allows teachers to provide better corrective instruction. The team should know more about students' misconceptions as they are reading students' answers to the questions.

In his book *Embedded Formative Assessment*, Dylan Wiliam (2011) suggests the following definition for formative assessment, which affirms this thinking:

> An assessment functions formatively to the extent that evidence about student achievement is elicited, interpreted, and used by teachers, learners, or their peers to make decisions about the next steps in instruction that are likely to be better, or better founded, than the decisions they would have made in the absence of that evidence. (p. 43)

Understanding that formative assessments can expose students' thinking about why they believe an answer is correct helps teams more enthusiastically pursue the work involved. Having a protocol for this work is also beneficial for teams. Consider the protocol we have developed for using common formative assessment data in table 6.2 (page 82).

Table 6.1: Protocol for Using Common Summative Assessment Data

Steps	Team Notes
1. Set the stage. • Establish the purpose of the meeting. • Determine the desired outcome. • Review norms (focusing on data norms).	Three minutes
2. Review the focus of the assessment, addressing the following questions. • How are the data from this assessment organized? • What learning targets or standards were measured? • How do we determine proficiency?	Five minutes Ensure input from all participants.

3. Discuss the data.
 	
• Working individually, each teacher should examine the data, looking for fact statements and not drawing any inferences or conclusions.
• Take turns sharing the facts; the recorder takes notes.
• Once everyone has listed the facts, the group then begins to develop inferences and conclusions.
   • How many students were proficient, not proficient, and beyond proficient?
   • Discuss patterns in the data such as how clusters of students (by subgroup, by teacher) performed, how any specific interventions affected growth, and how changes in pacing or instructional strategies affected performance.
• If we are using this assessment for screening or progress monitoring, identify the students who need continued support and those who need less support.
	Fifteen to twenty minutes
	
	Record the facts first and then the inferences and conclusions.

4. Develop the action plan. • Develop the plans for how to use the data to work with flexible student groups, change pacing if needed, and consider any instructional strategies to add.	Fifteen to twenty minutes
5. Set goals for improvement. • Discuss what we learned from these data and what follow-up assessments we will use. • Consider any obstacles or stumbling blocks the discussion identified. • Discuss ongoing efforts and strategies designed to ensure quality initial instruction. • If appropriate, review the SMART goal this assessment measures, and tweak as necessary.	Eight to ten minutes Identify no more than three strategies to directly impact achievement in this area.
6. Determine agreed-on actions and results indicators. • What indicators will we use to determine the effectiveness of the results of this action plan? • How will we know if this plan is effectively improving student achievement?	Five minutes Record decisions and summarize for the group.

*Visit **go.SolutionTree.com/assessment** for a free reproducible version of this table.*

Table 6.2: Protocol for Using Common Formative Assessment Data

Steps	Team Notes
1. Set the stage. • Establish the purpose of the meeting. • Review norms (focusing on data norms).	Two minutes
2. Review the focus of the assessment. • Identify the essential learning targets we assessed and which questions we designed to assess each of them. • Review the expectations for proficiency (for example, two out of three correct on a multiple-choice assessment, or a level 3 on the rubric). • Discuss any questions we had when we scored student work.	Two minutes
3. Discuss the data. • For each target, identify how many students will need additional time and support.	Five minutes Each team member must participate in this discussion.
4. Determine student misconceptions and errors. • For each target, identify which students need help. • Once we've identified the students who need help, regroup them by specific need (for example, students who made a calculation error versus students who chose the wrong solution pathway).	Ten minutes Be careful to do this step one essential learning target at a time.
5. Determine instructional strategies. • Decide whether we will develop small groups for reteaching or if we will use a re-engagement lesson with the whole class. • Each teacher should share his or her original instructional strategy so that we can see if one strategy worked better for certain students. • For each target and for each mistake or misconception, develop a plan to help students move ahead on their learning of that target. • If necessary, go back to best practice information about how to teach the concept or about what strategies work best for struggling students. Consult instructional coaches or specialists if necessary.	Fifteen minutes Make sure that all team members have the same understanding of what this will look like.
6. Develop the items that we will use to monitor whether students met the learning target after this response. This will provide information about which students still need help on this essential target.	Ten minutes This reassessment may be done orally or may be a version of the original assessment.

Visit go.SolutionTree.com/assessment for a free reproducible version of this table.

Step 1 in the data protocol asks the team members to review the purpose of the meeting and any data norms that they have established. During step 2 the team members review the essential learning targets they have assessed and what proficiency they required for each target, for example, a score of 3 on the rubric, or two out of three multiple-choice questions correct.

During step 3, the team examines each essential learning target and provides the number of students who fell into each level of proficiency for that target. This step helps the team see the big picture of their data. If they have only a few students who haven't reached proficiency, for example, they may decide to pull all of those students together for corrective instruction. Or, if they have many students who are not yet proficient, they may decide to have each teacher keep his or her students in their original classroom setting and use a common strategy for the corrective instruction.

When moving to step 4 in the protocol, teachers will use the actual student responses to learn more about what students still need. During this step, the team's goal is to recognize the specific mistakes students make or misconceptions students have about an essential learning target. Consider how this could work if teachers start with target 1 and create two piles of student work—those that demonstrate proficiency and those that do not. Then they take the second pile and distribute student work by what was incorrect about their answers. This step in the protocol is more effective when the assessment has asked students to explain their reasoning and with constructed-response questions. We'll explore this step later in this chapter, but for now, it's important to recognize that there may be more than one reason a student hasn't yet learned the target, or more than one step in a progression where their learning has stopped.

Planning the response occurs during step 5. Using the evidence of what misunderstandings students have about a learning target, or about where their learning stopped in a progression, the team plans the corrective instruction for those students. Sometimes teams will create smaller student groups for reteaching and at other times they may keep the group together for a re-engagement lesson. Teachers share their original instructional strategies to see if there are one or more strategies that were most effective with a particular group of students. Additionally, the team members must plan what they will ask their proficient students to do to extend their learning. If the team struggles with next steps, it may go back to best practice information or consult coaches or specialists for insight. It will also decide whether to share students across the team or have each teacher keep his or her students. If teachers plan to share students, they decide which teacher will work with each group.

Planning how the team will reassess nonproficient students after the corrective instruction occurs during step 6. This reassessment might be the same assessment previously used if the students won't remember the questions and answers, it may be an alternate version of the first assessment, or the teacher can ask students questions orally to determine if the extra help is enough for each student. We acknowledge that, even with additional time and support, some students may not yet be proficient. This reassessment identifies these students, and these students then move into a Tier 2 intervention.

Analyzing Results

So, how can a team most effectively analyze the results from a common formative assessment to develop a strong response for students? We've generalized the process into three different strategies based on the type of assessment items the team is using: (1) understand the learning progression, (2) pile and plan, and (3) conduct error analysis. In addition to these strategies, we include a list of common data-analysis mistakes we've seen that we caution teams to avoid.

Understand the Learning Progression

Teams may use this strategy while they unwrap their standards or they may wait until they have data to employ it. W. James Popham (2008) defines a *learning progression* as a carefully "sequenced set of subskills and bodies of knowledge it is believed students must master en route to mastering a more remote curricular aim" (p. 47). When teams use learning progressions in their assessment work, they begin with the expected learning target (often called the *proficiency target*), as well as the prerequisite targets. They bookend the progression with the knowledge and concepts students should already have and what mastery of the target will look like. The team defines any lower-level targets that students must master in between and an extended target, if appropriate. The prerequisite target is either from the previous year or course or from earlier in the current year.

Consider how this might look for a fourth-grade team teaching the proficiency target "Compare and contrast a firsthand and secondhand account of the same event or topic" (RI.4.6; NGA & CCSSO, 2010a). The team starts with the expected third-grade target (prerequisite skill) as one bookend, and this fourth-grade target as the other bookend. Team members determine what simpler targets the student must master in between to be able to meet the proficiency target. In this case, the student must be able to define the terms *firsthand account* and *secondhand account* and must also be able to discern whether a piece of text is a firsthand or secondhand account. See figure 6.1 for an illustration of the learning progression for this target.

Bookend		Bookend	
Prerequisite Target	Simpler Targets	Proficiency Target	Extended Target
Distinguish their own point of view from that of the author of the text. (RI.3.6)	1. Understand the terms *firsthand account* and *secondhand account*. 2. Identify whether a text is written from a firsthand or secondhand point of view.	Compare and contrast a firsthand and secondhand account of the same event or topic. (RI.4.6)	Revise a piece of text written as a secondhand account to make it a firsthand account or vice versa.

Figure 6.1: Example of a learning progression for comparing and contrasting points of view.

By using a learning progression, the team can examine the student responses to determine where the student learning stopped. It can then develop very specific corrective instruction. In this fourth-grade example, the team might realize that some of its students cannot accomplish either of the simpler targets, meaning the teachers must reteach them both. Other students might know the terms but need more practice in identifying the text's point of view. The team might develop two different corrective instructional strategies as a result.

Figure 6.2 provides an additional example based on a target for a high school U.S. history class based on the History–Social Science Content Standards for California Public Schools (California Department of Education, 2000).

Bookend		Bookend	
Prerequisite Target	Simpler Targets	Proficiency Target	Extended Target
Analyze the causes of the Cold War. (10.9.2)	1. Know the powers the president is granted in the Constitution. 2. Understand executive privilege, inherent power, and delegation of power as it relates to the president.	Describe the increased power of the presidency in response to the Cold War. (11.8.5)	Evaluate how the president's power is currently being used and how it has increased over time.

Figure 6.2: Example of a learning progression for U.S. history.

Developing a learning progression can help teachers both with instruction as well as assessment. The process helps teachers diagnose specifically where a student's learning has broken down. This specificity improves corrective instruction and makes it much more likely to help students learn the proficiency targets. Teams can use this strategy with all types of questions: selected response, constructed response, performance, and performance tasks.

Pile and Plan

Earlier in this chapter, we discussed a team of teachers dividing student work into piles to understand the data. This strategy is most effective when teams are examining constructed-response items, performance items, or performance task items because these help expose what the student was thinking with his or her answer. We call this the pile and plan method, because teachers start with a specific learning target they want to analyze and make two piles of student responses: correct and incorrect. Once they have all the incorrect student responses in one pile, they can regroup the student work into smaller piles with different student mistakes or misconceptions in each pile.

For example, consider this SBAC mathematics problem assessing the learning target "Solve word problems involving multiplication of a fraction by a whole number" (4.NF.B.4.C):

> Liam is making lemonade. He needs 16 ounces of lemon juice. He has 10 lemons.
>
> Each lemon makes about 1½ ounces of lemon juice. Will he have enough lemon juice? Explain how you know. (SBAC, 2014, p. 4)

When making piles, the team realizes that there are three stacks of student responses. In the first pile, students answer the problem using the correct solution pathway (multiplying 10 × 1½ and then seeing if it is equal to or greater than 16) that should get them to the correct answer but make a calculation error in the work. Another pile includes students who have chosen an incorrect solution pathway (multiplying 10 × 1 and then adding ½) that results in an incorrect answer. The third pile contains student answers that use the correct solution pathway and get the correct answer.

In this case, the team must develop a corrective instructional strategy to use with three different groups. The first group is the students who made a calculation error. The team decides to choose three different student responses with calculation errors and have cooperative groups work together to find the errors. After practicing the process with precision, these students receive another similar problem as a reassessment to see if they can now solve it correctly.

The second group of students needs more practice with multiplying whole numbers and fractions. The team sets up several different realistic problems using this process and employs manipulatives to make the concept more concrete. Again, after some practice with manipulatives, the students receive another similar problem to solve to see if they've mastered it.

The third group is the students who solved the problem accurately. The collaborative team wants to extend its learning on this target. It decides to put these students into cooperative groups and ask them to respond to additional word problems the team has created that require students to multiply whole numbers and fractions.

Conduct Error Analysis

Error analysis works best for multiple-choice items. With this strategy, the team examines student answers to multiple-choice questions. Kopriva (2008, p. 8) provides a clear example with the following question for the learning target: "The student can solve real-world problems using the greatest common divisor."

> Joseph is trying to distribute daffodils and tulips among vases so that each vase has the same number of daffodils and each vase has the same number of tulips. If there are 126 daffodils and 210 tulips and all were used, what is the greatest number of vases that Joseph can assemble? Select your answer and show your work.
>
>   (a) 7
>
>   (b) 14
>
>   (c) 42
>
>   (d) 84

The team chose these answer choices to reveal what students were likely thinking when they made their selections. For example, choice *a* is the largest prime number that can be divided into both numbers and represents a common student misconception. In this case, corrective instruction would include examples that use the largest prime number and those that use the greatest common divisor so students can see the difference. Choice *d* is the answer students get if they subtract the two numbers. This is, of course, the wrong solution pathway, and the corrective instruction for these students would likely include several different problems related to the learning target. The teacher might provide problems in which the student has to find the greatest common divisor and also problems that don't use this concept to help their students know when it's appropriate to use.

This strategy can also work with questions in other content areas. Consider, for example, a question from California's grade 5 Science Standards Test (California Department of Education, 2009, p. 11):

> A metal spoon was left in a pot of boiling soup. The cook burned a finger by touching the spoon. Why did the finger get burned?
>
>   A The metal spoon chemically reacted with the cook's hand.
>
>   B The metal spoon conducted electricity to the cook's hand.
>
>   C The metal spoon conducted heat to the cook's hand.
>
>   D The metal spoon insulated the cook's hand.

In this case, choice *a* would indicate that the student didn't understand the difference between chemical and physical properties. The corrective instruction would likely include some discussion about the differences and examples of both types of properties and why this situation didn't involve a chemical change. Students who chose *b* very likely didn't understand what the question was asking. They had some understanding that a person can get burned with electricity and made a poor guess. Students who chose *d* likely didn't understand the difference between insulation and conduction. In this corrective instruction lesson, students would review the vocabulary and receive specific information about the differences between the two terms.

When using this process, teams must write the multiple-choice question with specific wrong answer choices (distractors) that allow them to see where the students went wrong in their thinking.

Avoid Common Mistakes

As we've worked with teams in using common formative assessment data, we've identified some common mistakes. We list a few of these practices to avoid so that readers may simultaneously learn from others' mistakes and avoid making these same mistakes themselves.

- You should *not* average data across the learning targets you're assessing. If a student is beyond proficiency on one target and not yet proficient on another, it doesn't matter if the average is proficient. This student still needs help on the second learning target.

- You should *not* average the scores of all the students in a class or all the students on a team. Even if only one student has yet to master an essential target, this student needs corrective instruction.

- You should *not* make excuses about the data. Consider this common statement we hear: "I have an inclusion class, so you can't expect my class's scores to be as high as everyone else's." If we truly believe that all students can learn at high levels, we shouldn't be giving ourselves permission to let some fail.

- You should *not* draw conclusions that aren't based on facts. We sometimes hear statements like, "My kids don't like to write. They probably just wrote anything down to be done with it." Working with facts helps your team stay on the correct instructional path.

- Teachers should *not* analyze and respond to data independently. We've seen teams, in an effort to save time, direct each teacher to score his or her own student work and respond in his or her own classroom. This usually occurs when teachers feel pressured by time and want to respond as quickly as possible. However, with a common formative assessment, the value of the collaborative process in analyzing students' mistakes and in planning effective responses should make finding the time to work together a priority. We've also seen team meetings where teachers have scored their student work differently; they accepted or rejected certain answers, or awarded or deducted points for a variety of different reasons. As we discussed in chapter 5, to avoid these mistakes, it is important that the team develops an answer key with correct answers and anticipated incorrect answers.

Developing the Instructional Response

The most common ways teams develop a response to the data from a common formative assessment are by creating differentiated groups of students and planning a specific lesson for each of those groups designed to overcome the mistake or misunderstanding the assessment data reveal. It is crucial that the instructional practice used for the response is not the same as the initial instruction, and this is one of the advantages of using a team to develop the response. When teams share their initial instructional strategies, members often hear about multiple ways to teach a concept. Students benefit from the opportunity to learn in a much smaller group setting, as it provides instant and specific feedback for each student.

Every subject area has different ways for teachers to change instruction for students who experienced difficulty after initial instruction. For example, using manipulatives to make a concept more concrete, providing examples and nonexamples to help students see the concept more clearly, teaching specific scaffolding strategies such as chunking the text, using graphic organizers, having videos available for students who want to see the concept taught one more time, and so on. The value of the collaborative team is that the various members often can share ideas that not everyone has used before.

Responding Within the RTI Framework

RTI is the way that schools plan a multiple tiered approach to support all students in their learning. It is focused on quality core instruction with multiple additional levels of support when needed. In their book *Simplifying Response to Intervention*, Austin Buffum, Mike Mattos, and Chris Weber (2012) describe how collaborative teams respond when students experience difficulty learning. They explain how the amount of support a student needs will change over time and how important it is for teams to accurately use assessment results to guide this work.

The RTI framework is how collaborative teams in a professional learning community answer critical questions three and four: What will we do for the students who need more time and support? and What will we do for students who can already do the work? The pyramid reflects the anticipated ways that a school can build this response. The top level is Tier 1 and represents the support most students will need in order to be proficient on grade-level curriculum. That is, most students should be proficient with the core curriculum—instruction on essential standards and using common formative assessments to determine what additional support students need in the classroom. Tier 2 represents the amount of targeted support some students will need to be proficient on grade-level curriculum—additional small-group support usually two or three times a week for a period of time. Tier 3 represents the intensive support a small number of students will need either one-to-one or in a small group.

Figure 6.3 depicts the RTI structure.

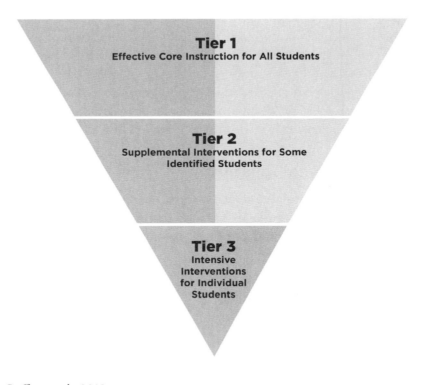

Source: Adapted from Buffum et al., 2012.

Figure 6.3: The inverted RTI pyramid.

Tier 1 teaching is called *core instruction* because it includes the guaranteed and viable curriculum for a specific grade level or course. For example, in algebra 1, the core curriculum includes all algebra 1 essential standards and learning targets. During the instructional process, the algebra 1 teachers use common formative assessments written around the essential learning targets for their course to determine which students have mastered them and which have not. When students haven't yet mastered an essential learning target, the teachers respond immediately, during their regular instructional time, to make sure students have learned the essential curriculum. The reality is, however, that there will likely still be students who will need more help even after they have had this extra dose of instruction. In this case, the students receive Tier 2 support.

We intend core instruction (Tier 1) to ensure that approximately 80–85 percent of students master the essential standards for the course or grade level. That is, schools will have that percentage of proficient students on the state test. However, many schools we've worked with have percentage rates of proficient students that are lower than this. It is extremely difficult to support more than 15–20 percent of students in an intervention system that provides students with more time and smaller groups around individual learning targets and standards. While many schools have developed elaborate response pyramids, it becomes extremely important for teams in these schools to strengthen their core instruction model with effective common formative assessments and corrective instruction so they can increase the number of students who are learning with core instruction. While we know it's urgent to develop strong models to support students below grade level, we also know that we'll never close the gap without a focus on quality core instruction and common formative assessment.

When teams have assessed essential learning targets in a common formative assessment and have provided additional support in the classroom, they must reassess those learning targets to make sure students are now proficient. If they are still not yet proficient, these students will be provided a Tier 2 response around the identified essential targets. This student receives additional help in a smaller group two to three times per week. His or her progress is monitored so that when proficient, she or he is no longer in this extra intervention time.

To continue our algebra example, we know that some students will enter algebra 1 classrooms without all of the important prerequisite skills for this course. These students will need more than just the core algebra 1 curriculum in order to fill in the gaps for prerequisite learning. Teams should fill those gaps in with Tier 3 intensive support that occurs when no new core instruction is taking place. Teachers can use a variety of assessments to determine what those gaps include: information provided by the previous year's teacher, a universal screener, a summative assessment or preassessment of the previous year's work, or state or benchmark assessment information. Notice that these assessments are summative in nature and written around learning targets and standards from the curriculum students should already know. By effectively using a balanced assessment system that provides the information teams need to make decisions, teams can increase student learning.

Table 6.3 (page 90) reflects different types of assessments within each RTI tier that can yield actionable data about student needs or prerequisites students require. These assessments support teachers' responses for students.

Table 6.3: Assessment Types Within the RTI Structure

Tier	Assessment
3	Universal screener, state test, progress-monitoring tools, and benchmarks
2	Benchmarks, progress-monitoring tools, assessments after corrective instruction, and common summative assessments
1	Common formative assessments and classroom formative assessments

Administering Re-Engagement Lessons

After a team gives a common formative assessment, it may decide that rather than pulling small groups together for additional time and support, the most effective way to respond to the results is by using a re-engagement lesson with the entire class. We first learned about re-engagement lessons from our mathematics colleagues. These lessons respond to common formative assessment data by keeping the entire class together rather than working with students in smaller differentiated groups. Teachers organize students into heterogeneous collaborative groups to work together as they investigate a particular problem using several guiding questions about the learning targets that they assessed. This strategy benefits even students who have reached proficiency on the target because they see other solutions or answers that were also correct and can expand their own knowledge of the learning target. Meanwhile, students who have not yet reached proficiency see a variety of ways to answer the question and can hear from their peers about how to do it. Collaborative teams who want to increase and improve student discourse achieve this goal because students work for much of the lesson in small groups, building on the thinking of each other. The teacher's role during this time is to help teams move forward if they get stuck by asking advancing questions. Teams can plan these questions as they hold their data team meetings to look at assessment results.

While there are many references to re-engagement lessons in mathematics literature (Briars, Asturias, Foster, & Gale, 2013; Charles A. Dana Center, 2016), we have extended the process to other content areas in our work with teams. It's important for teams to understand how reteaching and re-engagement differ. Table 6.4 highlights the major differences.

Table 6.4: Reteaching Versus Re-Engagement

Reteaching	Re-Engagement
Teach standards in the unit again in the same way as the original presentation.	Revisit student thinking using focused tasks that represent content standards for the unit.
Address basic skills that are missing.	Address conceptual understanding that is missing.
Do the same or similar problems over.	Examine the same or new tasks or different perspectives.
Practice more to make sure students learn the procedures.	Critique student approaches and solutions to make connections to the tasks.
Focus mostly on students in need of additional support.	Focus on engaging both students in need of support and students in need of enrichment.
Lower students' cognitive-demand expectations.	Raise students' cognitive-demand expectations.

Source: Adapted from Briars et al., 2013.

Typically, a group of students works with three or four sample student responses from the common formative assessment, which usually include at least two correct responses and may include incorrect responses. The teacher guides the groups through the lesson by using specific questions that help uncover their explanations for solving the problem. Consider the five-step protocol we have developed for creating a re-engagement lesson.

- **Step 1:** Determine if a re-engagement lesson will work in this situation. For example, there must be learning targets that allow multiple right answers or solution pathways. The student work from the assessment must contain at least two strong examples of correct answers that the student groups can compare.

- **Step 2:** The team determines which learning targets it will emphasize during the re-engagement lesson and identifies at least two student work samples it will use.

- **Step 3:** The team designs the lesson considering how large the groups will be, what it will ask groups to do, what questions it will ask, and how and when whole-group instruction will occur. The team plans how to begin the lesson, and it writes the initial questions or prompts. For example: "Examine these two answers from different students to make sense of their thinking and the strategy they used. Compare their responses and decide if they are correct or incorrect."

- **Step 4:** The team develops strong questions (assessing and advancing) that it can pose to assist student groups who might get stuck or to ensure students make progress throughout the lesson.

- **Step 5:** The team plans how it will reassess students at the end of the lesson to determine whether the students who were not yet proficient prior to this lesson have reached proficiency.

Reassessing After the Response

It is important that we know, after students have received additional time and support, if they have mastered the essential learning targets that we assessed. To this end, the team must develop a new assessment. This assessment might be an alternate version of the original assessment, an oral assessment the teacher uses immediately following the response, or a totally new assessment. We know that realistically, there will likely be some students who are still not proficient even after this extra time and support. These students will then receive a Tier 2 response such as a lesson that focuses on the simpler concepts the students need to know (see the section Understand the Learning Progression in this chapter [pages 83–85]) or one focused on the misconception or misunderstanding identified through the pile and plan or error analysis strategies.

As we stated in previous chapters, it's important for teams to take some time to reflect on their work. In looking at this step of the assessment process, however, the results might not always be immediately apparent because not all students will have reached proficiency. However, teams can consider the effectiveness of their timing and implementation of responses. They can also consider how many students were proficient as a result of Tier 1 instruction and support.

Conclusion

A team can more easily plan a quality response when it creates an assessment which is based on the essential learning targets being assessed, when items are chosen to match the rigor of that learning target, and when they can use the students' work to develop the specific responses students need.

TIPS FOR TRACTION

- Be crystal clear about the purpose of the assessment data you're using. If they're to guide instruction, make sure the data have a small enough grain size (learning target) to be able to develop a specific instructional response. If they're to measure the effectiveness of pacing, curriculum, or instruction, a larger grain size (standard) will serve you better.

- Choose the type of data analysis that matches the assessment items the best: learning progression, pile and plan, or error analysis.

- For corrective instruction, make sure you know, student by student and target by target, who has and has not yet reached mastery.

- Protocols help you keep your team discussions on track, allow you to better use your time, and help you negotiate more difficult topics, such as which instructional strategy worked best.

- Use the response strategy (learning progression, pile and plan, error analysis) that best matches the assessment you've used.

- If your data show that you have less than 80–85 percent of students achieving at proficiency level, make sure you focus on core instructional strategies that work. Common formative assessments guide this core instruction.

CHAPTER 7

Focusing on Feedback and Grappling With Grading

COMMON QUESTIONS AND CHALLENGES

- Should we be grading common formative assessments?
- Aren't students just worried about getting a grade?
- How do we keep track of how students are doing if we don't provide a grade?
- How many chances should students have before they get a grade?
- How can we include students in the assessment process?

As we clarified in chapter 1, teams use common formative assessments to identify:

> (1) individual students who need additional time and support for learning, (2) the teaching strategies that proved effective in helping students acquire the intended knowledge and skills, (3) program concerns—areas in which students generally are having difficulty achieving the intended standard—and (4) improvement goals for individual teachers and the team. (DuFour, DuFour, Eaker, & Many, 2010, p. 63)

Notably missing from this list is the goal of assigning a grade to students, and we completely agree that it should not be included here. Let us be clear that while we recognize the need for teams to utilize data to determine student grades, the primary purpose of data from common formative assessments is to support student learning.

However, a goal we think teams *should* add as a reminder is the opportunity to provide meaningful and timely feedback to students. Teachers and students can maximize the power of data from a formative assessment when they both use it during the learning process to *improve* learning (Popham, 2008). John Hattie (1999) states, "The most powerful single moderator that enhances learning achievement is feedback" (p. 9), and his research ranks feedback among the top-ten factors that contribute to learning (Hattie, 2009). Conversely, when teachers impose grades during this learning process, feedback goes largely unused, and we actually can see learning decline (Butler & Nisan, 1986; Lipnevich & Smith, 2008).

The powerful role that feedback can play in student achievement is clear. While teachers and teams typically use assessments to provide feedback on their students' learning, they may not naturally bring students into the loop. We see many teachers and teams struggle with how they can involve students in a practical and doable way, as well as with the notion of using assessments in a way that goes beyond traditional grading and serves to increase learning. This chapter presents guidelines and strategies to help teams more successfully use the power of feedback, with specific emphasis on including students.

Foster a Learning Partnership With Students

One of our favorite definitions of formative assessment comes from Popham (2008): "Formative assessment is a planned process in which assessment-elicited evidence of students' status is used by teachers to adjust their ongoing instructional procedures or by students to adjust their current learning tactics" (p. 112). Popham's (2008) definition implies that students are actively part of the process and should be routinely involved with examining evidence of their learning throughout instruction. They, along with teacher teams, should make decisions based on evidence and feedback from formative assessments focused on essential learning targets.

Popham (2008) describes four levels or categories of formative assessment implementation: (1) teachers' instructional adjustments, (2) students' learning tactic adjustments, (3) classroom climate shift, and (4) schoolwide implementation. He presents these levels of implementation as a guide for schools as they implement quality assessment practices and notes that teams may intentionally address them out of sequence depending on current practices. Following are descriptions of each level (Popham, 2008).

- **Level 1: Teachers' instructional adjustments**—In this level, teachers collect assessment evidence and use it to decide whether to adjust their current or immediately upcoming instruction in order to improve its effectiveness.

- **Level 2: Students' learning tactic adjustments**—When classrooms are at level 2, students rely on assessment evidence regarding their current skills and knowledge status to decide whether to adjust the procedures they use when trying to learn something.

- **Level 3: Classroom climate shift**—At this level, there is a clear culture within the classroom that reflects a fundamental change in the teacher's and students' (1) learning expectations, (2) perceptions about who is responsible for students' learning, and (3) attitude about the role of classroom assessment. Students view themselves as partners in the process and own their learning.

- **Level 4: Schoolwide implementation**—When an entire school or a district adopts one or more levels of formative assessment, typically via professional development or the implementation of the professional learning community process, they reflect level 4.

The classroom culture Popham (2008) describes is a dependent partnership between teachers and students who possess a growth mindset. These teachers acknowledge that their students enter their classrooms with a variety of backgrounds and skills, yet they must work with the relentless belief that even though students might need additional time and support, they can still achieve high levels of learning. They engage students in the discussion of learning targets and quality work. They use data as sources of evidence that guide that additional support and continual focus on increasing learning, and they interact in a productive way with students using those data as a vehicle for improvement. Students in this kind of classroom culture know that the ultimate goal is learning (versus grading) and view assessments as an opportunity to receive feedback on that learning. Teachers empower them with clear targets for the knowledge and skills they must gain and demonstrate. They know that while they may not yet have certain skills or quality in their work, they believe that through the use of strategies and feedback from their assessments, they can continue to grow.

In a learning partnership, teachers make sure their class knows its role is to ensure student learning and help them throughout the process to achieve that goal. Students see themselves as partners with their teachers in this endeavor and embrace their roles and responsibilities. The classroom functions with the spirit of collaboration rather than competition and the common goal of getting all students to high levels of achievement.

We see a parallel between what teams and students need to be successful in meeting learning goals. Figure 7.1 illustrates this concept.

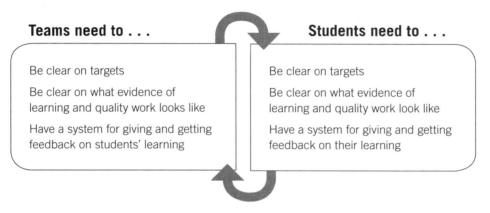

Figure 7.1: Teams' and students' needs for success.

Just like teachers, students need to be clear on their targets. They need to know what quality work looks like. In classrooms with a culture of partnership for learning, teachers clearly communicate this information as well as how they will use assessments—not as "gotchas" but as sources of evidence to learn what students know and can do. If the goal is to improve student learning, teachers must include them in the system of getting and using feedback.

Student Involvement in the Assessment Process

In *Common Formative Assessment* (Bailey & Jakicic, 2012), we emphasized the importance of including students in the assessment process. Numerous studies reveal the value of this practice, and we think it's important enough to remind readers of the power inherent in it. We assert that the engagement of students throughout the assessment process not only raises student achievement (Black & Wiliam, 1998; Hattie, 2012) but also powerfully propels students to own their learning. Students who are clear on their strengths and areas of need are more likely to believe in their potential to develop their abilities and continually improve (Dweck, 2008).

As part of the backward-planning process, teams can intentionally embed specific experiences for students that build their knowledge of:

- The individual targets for learning, including what success looks like

- The elements of quality within any product that teachers will expect them to produce
- Their current level of proficiency or quality of work on the target, based on feedback from a variety of sources
- Specific learning tactics they can use to enhance their proficiency and quality of work

The following scenario illustrates how a team might engage in this process to improve student engagement.

Team Scenario for Planning Student Engagement

A sixth-grade team has been planning a unit of study in which teachers will expect students to write arguments to support claims with clear reasons and relevant evidence. While identifying learning targets, they quickly convert them into student-friendly "I can" statements so students know what they will learn throughout the unit. As the team designs its learning plan, it embeds activities that will engage students in examining and actively working with an argument-writing rubric. The team structures the first activity to have students work in teams to analyze anonymous student work. In this case, the student teams identify areas of strength and areas for enhancement or improvement in how the writer introduces the claim, organizes the evidence, and supports the claim with logical reasoning and evidence. Students will also examine annotated and scored anchor papers that highlight the rationale for the scores they earn, also based on the rubric. Later in the unit, students will individually examine their work, using the same rubric to gauge the quality of their writing based on the same parameters. Finally, they will participate in an editing process with a peer-to-peer "critical friend" protocol the course team designed to help gain insight into how their writing might improve. As follow-up, students will individually revise their writing in light of that feedback and then present their final draft to teachers with a self-evaluation of their work. This serves as the basis for a writing conference with the teacher in which the student plays an active role.

In this scenario, the team intentionally plans a unit to actively engage students in the process of getting, using, and communicating feedback on their learning. This powerful design promotes a sense of student ownership not only of their learning but also the quality of their work. It reinforces the growth mindset we want to support within all classrooms.

Clearly, establishing this type of culture within a classroom will not happen overnight. We know some of the shifts necessary to move to this culture will stretch the thinking of both teachers and students. We suggest that teams take time to examine the characteristics of classrooms that reflect true learning partnerships and commit to lead to their attainment. For example, team members might discuss how they will frame the use of formative assessments with all of their students at the beginning of the year. They will clearly communicate the role of formative assessments on the syllabus, share information with students and parents, and make decisions about the use of assessments in keeping with their new policy.

Focus on the Right Kind of Feedback

In order to maximize learning through feedback, both teachers and students must use the right kind of feedback. Effective feedback is timely and specific, and it guides students to adjust their learning plans or products. Rather than praising comments, such as "great paper" or "nice job," or those that are negative, such as "You can do better than this," students benefit from focused and specific feedback that steers them toward improvement, such as "I see the point you're trying to make, but I'd like to see more support for your reasoning. Can you give some more examples?"

Grant Wiggins (2012) offers several guidelines for providing effective feedback, which we believe serve as great reminders for teams. Among these, Wiggins (2012) recommends that feedback be *goal referenced*. In other words, it should relate to the goal for learning instead of something outside the purpose of the task. For example, if a student writes a paper to support a particular position or argument, the feedback should relate to the quality of that argument. Another key reminder is that feedback should be actionable and guide students toward strategies or tactics for improving. Vague comments such as "unclear" don't necessarily tell students to go back and reorganize a written passage. Feedback should be timely—too much delay between students' performance on a task and the feedback they receive increases the risk that they won't connect to or apply the feedback. We feel this is a major element of how valuable common formative assessments can be. Because they are brief, integrated measures of students' proficiency on skills and concepts during the instructional process, they can serve as tremendous vehicles for regular student feedback. Additionally, if common formative assessments contain effective constructed-response items, they lend themselves more readily to offering constructive feedback. While students can examine errors in their answers to selected-response items, it's more challenging to provide meaningful and specific feedback about the accuracy or quality of work through selected-response items.

Facilitate the Use of Feedback

One of the ways to promote student use of feedback is to guide them in how to use it. We can't assume that students will automatically welcome feedback, and unless we build in opportunities for them to apply it, they may not take advantage of its power. However, by intentionally building scaffolded steps into their instruction, teachers can gradually increase their students' ownership and use of feedback. Following is a suggested progression for empowering students to effectively use feedback.

- **Start safe, start small:** Rather than asking students to use their own work, engage students in situations where they examine an anonymous or generic piece of work against some indicator of quality, such as a rubric. For example, the teacher can present a piece of writing or a solved mathematics problem with a document camera to the class. Initially, students can watch the teacher conduct a think-aloud in which the teacher examines the work and provides feedback to the anonymous student, pausing to have students reflect on what they have just witnessed. We suggest focusing on a single aspect or characteristic to start so the process isn't overwhelming. For example, if you are asking students to examine a piece of informational writing, you may only have them look at how the author introduced the topic or whether the sequence of the piece was written effectively. Limiting the focus at first provides an opportunity for students to engage in the process without becoming overwhelmed by the content.

- **Build confidence through collaboration:** As a more advanced step in the process, students can work in teams with their peers to examine anonymous work and note the quality and accuracy of the work against a rubric or exemplar. Together, they can discuss the feedback they should provide about the quality or accuracy of the work, and the actions they would recommend for the anonymous student. Again, this provides a safe opportunity for students to learn the value of feedback and how it's used to improve a product's overall quality. It also reinforces the fact that everyone gets feedback on their work. It shouldn't be considered a negative, but an opportunity to grow.

- **Bring it home:** Once students are comfortable examining anonymous work and working with feedback, it's time to transition to that same practice using their own work. Again, we recommend examining at first a single aspect of the work that aligns to the focus of instruction and comparing it to familiar rubrics or exemplars. This most independent level reinforces our desire for students to generate feedback on their own work, and ultimately work in partnership with the teacher to incorporate feedback in a productive and meaningful way.

Foster Peer- and Self-Generated Feedback

Hattie (2009) explains that the highest level of learning takes place when students become their own teachers. In fact, his analysis of instructional practices points to the notion that student-generated feedback may, in fact, be more powerful than the feedback teachers provide. To that end, we want to help students own their learning. Rather than allowing students to depend on others to provide feedback on the quality and accuracy of their work, our goal is to empower students to use the tools and resources available to them to increase that quality with maximum independence. This means that over time, we need to transfer a greater amount of the responsibility to students. When we do this, we engage students further in examining their own work, conferencing with peers to solicit feedback, identifying specific actions to improve their work, and taking those actions to refine it. We are not implying that we simply transfer all responsibility to students in this process, but we certainly should increase the level of partnership between teachers and students.

How might we do this? Following are some specific activities teachers facilitate that enhance student ownership of feedback on the quality and accuracy of their work.

- **Have students co-craft rubrics:** Start with one aspect of quality at a time. Teachers can facilitate this as a whole-class activity or by dividing students into teams. Teachers present students with guiding questions to ensure that they consider all aspects of quality, and suggest language for students to include in a rubric.

- **Engage students in the identification of exemplars and anchor papers:** Anchor papers are examples of student work that represent different levels of quality or proficiency. For example, a team may collect papers representing the range of quality in a four-point writing rubric so that teachers and students have clarity on the characteristics. Exemplars are similar in that they are models that represent quality work.

  Teachers can give student teams anonymous scored papers such as essays, mathematics problems, or informational reports that represent various levels of quality to collaboratively examine, debate, and sort into proficiency levels based on a familiar rubric. During this time, the student teams look for evidence within the work to support or justify its level on the rubric. Once each team completes its determination, members can share the results of their findings with the rest of the class, supporting their decision with evidence. Once teams develop consensus across the classroom, post the papers as exemplars.

- **Structure peer-conferencing opportunities between students:** Although individual conferencing with students is something many teachers use within their classes, another option is to teach *peer-to-peer conferencing*—a structured time when students use the power of their peers to gain insights into the quality and accuracy of their work. Initially, students should be partnered with one other student for this activity. Provide students with a protocol for examining their peers' work to ensure their conversations are focused and productive. (See figure 7.2 for an example of a protocol that students can use for peer conferencing.) The protocol provides not only the process, but also clarifies the purpose of the work and expectations for the peer conference. Like any new routine, students should be initially guided in this process with modeling, examples, and practice. We also suggest that peer conferences begin with a focus or topic that is limited in scope, such as looking at a writer's word choice. Later, as students become more proficient and comfortable with a range of quality indicators, they can choose their own focus, asking their peers to provide feedback on a specific indicator.

Date of peer conference: _____

Partner names: _____

Feedback provider: _____

Product being reviewed: _____

Purpose of this process: The goal for peer feedback is to have another set of eyes so that we can improve our learning. When we work together and provide feedback, we learn specific ways to grow.

- We agree to be objective and base our comments and suggestions on evidence.

- We will keep an open mind about the feedback our partners give, and we will thank them for their time.

Step 1: Discuss the focus and plan for feedback. (Two minutes)

What is the focus of your feedback conversation? On what specific aspect or characteristic would your partner like feedback? What would be evidence of quality in this aspect? Is there a rubric or example of this quality that you could reference?

The focus of my feedback will be _____.

Step 2: Look at the work. (Five to ten minutes)

Look at your partner's work and identify evidence that focuses on the targeted area. (As an alternative, the partner may read the work to the peer reviewer.)

1. Use sticky notes or write in the margin to share your observations about the **strengths** of this work. Be specific about your feedback, using phrases such as *I liked how you . . .* or *This part was really effective because you . . .*

2. Identify one specific *suggestion* you would like to share with your partner about the focus area that will improve the quality of your partner's work. Remember, your suggestion should be based on evidence of the characteristic or aspect you are focusing on in the work. Following are some ways you might share your feedback.

   - I'm wondering if things might be clearer if . . .

   - One thing I noticed was . . .

   - Have you considered trying . . . ?

Step 3: The student responds to the feedback. (Three minutes)

Students can respond to the suggestions that were helpful and how they will use the suggestions to improve their work. Partners thank each other.

Figure 7.2: Peer-conferencing protocol.

Think Evidence, Not Grades

If students think the only purpose for showing what they know on formative assessments is to get a grade, they will not view the assessment as a potential source of useable, actionable feedback. We're certainly not saying that teachers shouldn't keep records of their students' achievement on formative measures. Quite the contrary. We believe this evidence is some of the most powerful information teachers can collect and share with the students, other teachers, and parents. But how we communicate that evidence is crucial. As an alternative to recording traditional letter grades or percentages, we suggest using a proficiency-based scoring system to record progress. In this way, teachers can document student scores in gradebooks as evidence of progress over time. The recorded evidence of proficiency can be viewed from a growth perspective rather than as a fixed record of performance. Consider using a four-point rubric, with a score of 3 reflecting proficiency. We like Marzano's (2010) proficiency scale definitions, which are based on the distinction between demonstration of simple versus complex concepts and skills. Following is a version of Marzano's (2010) four proficiency scale levels that we adapted (note that we've eliminated the 0 level Marzano includes).

4. In addition to exhibiting level 3 performance, the student makes in-depth inferences and applications that go *beyond* what was taught in class.

3. The student makes no major errors or omissions regarding any of the information or processes (simple or complex) that were explicitly taught.

2. The student makes no major errors or omissions regarding the simpler details and processes, *but* there are major errors or omissions regarding the more complex ideas and processes.

1. With *help*, the student shows a partial knowledge of some of the simpler and complex details and processes.

Many teams now use digital tools, such as Google Docs and other programs, to gather and analyze their data. Visit https://goo.gl/9lnWjN to access an example of a simple Google Form designed to monitor students' progress toward meeting an essential standard in kindergarten. The kindergarten team in this example constructed the form after unwrapping the standard. The team created a prompt for each of the learning targets and then developed a proficiency scale to score student responses. The language of the scoring scale is based on the Marzano scale language, with a 3 indicating proficiency.

A teacher can share such a form with all team members, and all can use it via any mobile device, such as a smartphone or tablet. As the teacher walks around the room and observes individual students, he or she can enter student names and responses to the questions or prompts into the form. These data then flow into an automatically created spreadsheet that can be sorted and analyzed by learning target and by student. Gathering these data enables teams to see student progress over time, and rather than averaging the scores, teams can analyze trends and patterns of proficiency. To learn more about using Google Forms, you can explore the Google Apps Learning Center at https://apps.google.com/learning-center/products /forms/get-started.

Discuss Grading and Scoring

While we've noted that assigning grades can dilute the power of formative assessments, we recognize that teams need to engage in meaningful dialogue around the various grading policies and practices used to reflect student learning on summative assessments, major projects, and even homework. While many districts have begun to explore alternatives to traditional grading, such as standards-based grading, they may initially start the conversation by looking at their existing practices to see if they are compatible with the assumptions we hold as a professional learning community. Among the questions teams frequently explore when entering these discussions are the following.

- Do we all use the same criteria for grades on major assignments and assessments? Should we allow students to retake summative assessments?

- How do we handle recording of information coming from formative assessments?

- How will we calculate grades if we don't factor in the formative assessments?

- Should we average scores or look at improvement?

In order to address these questions, teams should have constructive conversations in which they collectively (1) revisit team norms, (2) clarify the purpose of grading, and (3) consider what grading looks like in practice.

Revisit Team Norms

While we can share our beliefs and knowledge about grading as well as those of various education researchers such as Marzano (2010) and Susan Brookhart (2011), we also recognize that decisions must come from within the team, and that teams must reach those decisions after some level of discussion or debate. Whenever a team deals with a potentially loaded topic, which grading tends to be, we suggest revisiting its norms. Has the team established that it makes decisions by consensus? Does it prioritize student learning over teacher convenience? Do its norms ensure that all voices on the team will be heard? Before moving into any potential hotbed of debate, be sure to reach consensus on how team members will behave during the discussion.

Clarify the Purpose of Grading

We think a great place to begin any conversation about grading policy is to clarify the purpose of grading. Why are we providing grades in the first place? Brookhart (2011) shares some great focusing questions to begin the dialogue: "What meaning do we want our grades to convey? and Who is the primary intended audience for this message?" In considering these questions, team members' beliefs and potential misconceptions about grading begin to surface. Brookhart (2011) suggests providing this statement to members of the team:

> Grades are not about what students *earn*; they are about what students *learn*. To what degree do you and your colleagues believe that? If you do agree, what are the advantages to you and to your students? If you don't agree, why not?

Providing an opportunity for team members to voice their beliefs about grading and examine the *why* behind these practices often reveals that some of the traditional practices are incompatible with the beliefs inherent in a professional learning community. The ultimate goal of such an activity is to establish a collective set of beliefs among team members that will then steer any decision related to grading. In the next section, we provide the scenario of a middle school team engaged in the process of examining and building consensus around its grading and scoring practices.

Consider What Grading Looks Like in Practice

The nine members of the Newton Middle School mathematics team know they need to align their grading practices. They frequently receive feedback from administrators, parents, and students expressing concerns about the different grading practices each grade level uses and even among individual teachers within the grade levels. The areas of concern include the weighting of homework, the opportunity for students to retake assessments, and the handling of formative assessments.

The department chair, Angela Maxwell, meets with the members of the mathematics team and outlines the concerns. She shares that, as a department, members will engage in conversations related to their grading practices. The desired outcome of these conversations is that they will build consensus around grading practices that they will then uniformly implement departmentwide. She reinforces the fact that in the process of building consensus, each member will have the opportunity for input and that any decisions will be based on the will of the group.

To begin the process, Angela has the members review the norms they previously established and asks whether they suggest additions. One team member, Rob Daly, suggests that one norm they might consider is that the team should make decisions based on what is best for students. Another member, Greg London, asks that conversations include research regarding grading. After getting agreement from the rest of the members, the two norms are added.

Next, Angela poses the questions "Why do we grade?" and "What is our purpose?" Team members respond silently to the prompts by writing on sticky notes. After a period of time, the sticky notes are placed by each member on a piece of poster paper. As they are posted, two team members begin to cluster common responses together. Following is a summary of three common responses.

- To communicate information to students and parents about what they learned
- To make students accountable
- To motivate students to do better

As they get into deeper discussions around practices that support those purposes and those that are potentially incompatible, they realize they are sharing opinions rather than information supported by evidence. As big as some of the issues they would be tackling appear, members of the department agree that they might need to take small, incremental steps in the process of adopting new grading practices. They also recognize that because some team members are reluctant to examine some of the practices in light of their views, they need to ensure adequate time for everyone to consider and process the ideas.

Angela introduces the option for the team to take some time to build shared knowledge about standards-based grading. During the next few meetings, they collaboratively read articles Angela and other team members found about standards-based grading and related topics and summarize their learning. Members of the team can also bring examples of policies they found being used elsewhere.

After building shared knowledge over a few weeks, the team then decides it is time to tackle a single aspect of grading practices: policies related to formative measures. The specific questions they frame during the discussion include the following.

- Are students allowed to use their notes or mathematics journals during quizzes or other formative measures?
- Are retakes of quizzes and other formative measures allowed?

With their shared knowledge, they engage in a deeper study of the impact of allowing students to use their notes as well as retake quizzes and other formative measures, listing pros and cons related to student learning. In the end, they arrive at consensus that allowing students to use their notes and retake formative assessments will likely result in increased learning for students.

The team then generates a list of potential guidelines for practice that all members will formally adopt, and they reach consensus on the final wording. Following are the agreed-on guidelines they constructed.

- As a department, we will allow students to use their mathematics journals and notes during quizzes and other formative measures. We will not allow notes and journals during tests.

- Students will be able to retake formative assessments and receive half of a point for any corrections they make.

The middle school mathematics team we describe in this scenario is on a journey of examining its grading practices. Rather than being told how they should change their grading practices, the team members engage in collective conversations, facilitated by someone with the skill to guide conversations. While they have only tackled one aspect of grading, the team has moved forward with specific actions by building shared knowledge among members, reaching consensus, and relying on respectful norms. Team members have a strong foundation of collaborative decision making from which they can extend their own learning and continually adjust their practices as the journey progresses.

Conclusion

When teachers can foster an environment focused on learning instead of grades, students achieve more. When students are engaged as partners in this process, they learn more. There is plenty of evidence demonstrating a link between students' use of constructive, timely, and meaningful feedback and increases in learning. We encourage teams to collectively examine their practices. In their unit planning, teams can align their formative assessments with follow-up opportunities for students to actively engage in using feedback. By including intentional instruction using assessment information, they can build their students' comfort and confidence in using feedback to make adjustments in their learning tactics to improve their work's quality and accuracy. We also encourage teams to consider the grading practices that promote a growth mindset, creating a culture within their classrooms that values information coming from assessments so that students learn more and promotes a true partnership between teachers and students. By building this culture across classrooms within a team and across all teams within a school, teams will see a systemwide shift in which the focus is truly on learning.

TIPS FOR TRACTION

- As a grade-level team, build consensus around how you will monitor students' performance on formative measures. Remember to build your growth mindset around the power of "yet," and to use your formative measures for feedback.

- Consider using a proficiency-based scoring system instead of grades.

- Keep guidelines for providing quality feedback in mind.

- Intentionally plan for opportunities to engage students in the process of getting, giving, and using feedback to improve their learning.

CHAPTER 8

Using Common Assessments With Singleton Teachers

COMMON QUESTIONS AND CHALLENGES

- How can singleton teachers who don't have colleagues who teach the exact same content use common assessments in their work?
- Is there a way for interdisciplinary teams to use common assessments?

Collaborative teams in a professional learning community learn together. Building shared knowledge is always an important step in the process of coming to consensus about teams' decisions and conclusions. However, if that's all collaborative teams do, they will easily become stagnant. Many teams start building shared knowledge about the four critical questions of a PLC and even the research and literature about common assessments, but stop short of progressing to implementing what they have learned. If common formative assessments are the linchpin of a PLC, collaborative teams must become proficient in writing and using them, and the only way that can really happen is by trying out the process and learning from successes as well as mistakes. We consider assessment one of the hardest things that teams collaborate on, and for team members who don't teach the same content, it is even more complicated. Typically, these teams develop when a teacher is the only teacher in their school or district who teaches a particular grade level or course. We sometimes refer to these teachers as *singletons*. If the most common and best structure for collaborative team configuration is teachers who teach the same subject in the same school, we find that teachers who are singletons in their school or district and work in interdisciplinary teams, vertical teams, or electronic teams often struggle to develop *common* assessments (DuFour et al., 2016). These teachers struggle to determine what and how they can assess in a way to support students who need more time and support as well as how team members can learn from each other. In *Learning by Doing* (DuFour et al., 2016), the authors emphasize the importance of making sure teams are configured in a way that will allow them to engage in meaningful work, so finding solutions to the question of what's meaningful is an important first step.

So, if a team is configured to include teachers who don't teach a common set of standards, let's consider what common assessments look like in their setting. One of the hallmarks of a common formative assessment is that every teacher who teaches the same course or grade level administers it, and teachers learn together from the process. Singleton teachers worry that they don't have anyone to partner with to help them learn about effective assessment practices. Another hallmark of common formative assessments is that teams use the process to learn more about effective instructional strategies to teach specific learning targets, as well as ways to support students who need additional time and instruction. Teams who don't teach a common course or grade level wonder how they can tap into the power of common assessments. In fact, they often face the fact that, as William M. Ferriter (2010) puts it, "One of the greatest challenges in any professional learning community is finding meaningful learning partnerships for the singletons." Meaningful partnerships provide an opportunity for collaborative work that enhances the effectiveness of any one person and is more efficient than teachers working in isolation. Finding the right team structure and then pinpointing the right situations for common assessments are important if teams are to have meaningful partnerships. In this chapter, we'll tackle the ideas of what kinds of configurations work in developing common assessments for singleton teachers, and examine specifically how they can write assessments to produce data that can be used to support student learning, as well as how they respond to those data.

Configuring Teams

The first decision teams must make to build a meaningful partnership is how they will organize for the year. Who will work together to improve student learning? Typically, this decision happens before constructing the master schedule for the year so that team members can have common planning time. There are four general organizational structures that work for singletons: (1) vertical teams, (2) interdisciplinary teams, (3) cross-school and district teams, and (4) electronic teams.

Vertical Teams

Vertical teams organize themselves either around a grade span or a departmental subject (for example, K–3, 5–6, middle school science, or high school English language arts). This is probably the most common and effective team configuration for small schools and singletons, and it allows the team members to discuss both their content and their expectations for proficiency. This structure allows teams to have a common subject area (for example, mathematics, reading, or science), which is important as they begin to determine their essential standards and develop common assessments. While the teachers don't teach the exact same content (one teaches kindergarten reading, another first-grade reading, and so on), they will be able to share both instructional and assessment strategies.

There is no one right way to divide into teams; for example, we've worked with schools with K–1 teams, others with K–2 teams, and still others with K–3 teams. These teams should, however, decide they will work together because they have either a common subject (for example, mathematics) or a common grade span (for example, 3–5 or 6–8).

What's important is that the team has common planning time. Once the team members have established their meeting times, norms, and SMART goals, they can continue to work together or in a variety of smaller configurations throughout the school year, depending on the learning targets being assessed. For example, a vertical middle school English language arts team may decide to focus its team SMART goal around student writing. They work together to develop instructional strategies, anchor papers, and rubrics they will use to assess the writing standards. They may, however, break into smaller teams of just two grade levels when assessing essential standards that don't apply to all three grade levels.

Once teams have developed a pacing guide for each course or grade level, they look for overlapping essential standards—those standards that are about the same content or processes. This is where they write their common assessments. Remember that the entire team might not all have overlapping essential standards, but the team members can work in smaller configurations whenever appropriate.

The pacing guide may need tweaking so that a common assessment makes sense for a vertical team. Consider, for example, a high school social studies team in West Virginia that wants to assess the learning target "Distinguish among fact, opinion, and reasoned judgment in a text." In this state's tenth-grade college and career readiness standards for social studies, one of the essential targets in U.S history is, "Evaluate the impact of United States foreign policy on global affairs" (West Virginia Board of Education, n.d.). Eleventh grade has a related target in history: "Analyze United States isolationism, neutrality, and entanglement in world affairs" (West Virginia Board of Education, n.d.). Before the teachers of these two subjects develop their initial pacing guides, they teach these learning targets at two different times during the second semester, but the tenth-grade history teacher agrees to move the assessment for this target to a different unit in the second semester so that the two teachers can use a common assessment.

Interdisciplinary Teams

Interdisciplinary teams comprise teachers who have the same group of students but each teach a different subject (for example, a seventh-grade team made up of an English language arts, science, mathematics, and social studies teacher). These teams are frequently found in middle schools who create grade-level teams around a group of students, for example, the seventh-grade interdisciplinary team. They are also found in very small middle school and high schools where there is only one teacher in the entire school for each subject—mathematics, science, ELA, social studies, and so on. This team structure usually limits the common assessment topics to those that cross multiple subject areas, such as reading and writing, or to those that assess specific skills such as making inferences or analyzing a research topic.

Because these team members share students rather than content, they develop their assessments around either standards or common skills that cross into two or more subject areas. These teams start their work the same way as vertical teams: by identifying their essential standards and creating a pacing guide for when to teach them.

When an interdisciplinary team starts working on its common assessments, the members must first look for common skills and concepts. Since the Common Core English language arts standards cover science and technical subjects as well as history and social studies, they are an easy starting point for any interdisciplinary team. In addition, teams should consider 21st century skills, such as creativity, communication, and critical thinking, as well as skills that cross all subject areas, such as analyzing information, comparing and contrasting, and defending a claim.

Once the team members have identified what common skills they will teach and assess, they begin developing the assessment. Possibilities could include writing one assessment for the entire team to use, focusing on a couple of specific skills, giving the students several pieces of text and asking them to create a summary of the research from the texts, or having students compare two pieces of text to see which argument is the best supported. By using content-specific text pieces, teachers can consider the student work for mastery of both the English language arts and content-area learning targets.

Cross-School and District Teams

A third organizational structure is to have teams composed of teachers who are singletons in their own schools but who teach the same subject in different schools. These teams are often best supported in districts that have either early release or late start time schedules that allow teachers to travel between locations. For example, AP calculus teachers from two different high schools in the same school district meet collaboratively either in person or virtually during the early release time, or the only AP calculus teacher in one district might work with AP calculus teachers in another district. In an elementary district, the physical education teacher in an elementary school might work with other physical education teachers in the other elementary schools in the district. In a rural school district, there might be only one science teacher in their only middle school. This teacher might work with a science teacher in a neighboring middle school. In these cases, the team functions almost exactly as a collaborative team would in a more traditional setting. The only complications are making sure to build common time for planning into the master schedule for each school, and supporting travel between schools or electronic capability to work virtually.

Electronic Teams

Electronic teams are often a version of the cross-school or building configuration and occur when these team members are not able to meet in person. In most cases, electronic teams create common assessments the same way traditional teams do because they are going to collaborate with colleagues who teach the same content. Therefore, these teams can start their common assessment work by collaboratively choosing their essential standards, creating a pacing guide, and finding specific learning targets to assess.

There are, however, several issues that these teams will have to think about differently than their traditional team colleagues. The first is that they must find a common meeting time when all members can be online together. This means that more than one school schedule must provide time to work together. The second issue the team members must work out is how they will share their documents. Many schools have begun using Google Docs for sharing purposes, and this choice allows the team members to work on the documents at the same time. They can also use Google Hangouts for their online communication (Hansen, 2015). Finally, the team has to develop a way to share the results of its assessments with each member. This decision is complicated by the fact that members likely won't be able to share the actual student work as easily as teams who are in the same room. In these situations, creative solutions will have to be employed. For example, teachers might choose specific samples of student work that represent a common misunderstanding or misconception and upload a particular student response for the team to study, or they might spend some time together describing the responses of students who are proficient as well as those who aren't proficient.

Creating Common Assessments in Teams Configured Around Singletons

Once teams have chosen essential standards, the next step is to write and use common assessments, which will determine how to respond to students who haven't yet mastered the target as well as those who have mastered it and would benefit from enrichment. This is when teams have to explore how best to use common assessments in their own work.

Vertical Teams

We recommend vertical teams consider two ways of thinking about what they have in common: (1) specific skills that are the same and taught in each of their content areas or grades and (2) skills that are developed through a learning progression. These skills are similar but increase in complexity from one grade or course to the next.

Assess by Similar Skills

The first step in assessing similar skills is to determine the skills or concepts that courses or grade levels have in common that teams have identified as essential targets. Many vertical teams start with the ELA standards (in ELA, in science and technical subjects, and in history and social studies) because they have already been identified and the way they're laid out makes it easy to find connections among courses. For example, a third- through fifth-grade vertical team can examine the second Reading Standard for Informational Text across each grade to see how it builds from grade level to grade level (NGA & CCSSO, 2010a). For the sixth- through eighth-grade science team in a middle school, members are all working toward a common set of reading and writing standards in science and technical subjects. They can use any of these that they identify as essential standards to write their common formative or summative assessments.

Beyond ELA, there are many other skills that teams can commonly assess. In the Common Core mathematics standards, there are several learning progressions that cross grade levels (see http://math .arizona.edu/~ime/progressions for some good examples). For example, fractions are taught in third through fifth grade. Teachers can work together to develop assessments that reflect these progressions. Although the specific fraction skills being assessed will vary by grade level, the types of questions used can be the same. The other common skills that cross all grades or courses in mathematics are the eight Standards for Mathematical Practice (NGA & CCSSO, 2010b; also see pages 25–26 in this book). We've worked with vertical teams who develop specific ways to assess the mathematical practices in their common assessments.

In our experience, once the teams have looked carefully at their standards, they will find many other skills that they have in common. These include 21st century skills such as communication and creative and critical thinking, as well as asking questions and solving problems, carrying out a plan, explaining a process, looking for patterns, developing an argument, and understanding data tables, charts, and graphs. No one content area is usually charged with teaching these broader concepts, and vertical teams use these skills for their common assessments.

In the following sections, we share three examples of vertical teams assessing by similar skills in each one of their classes. You'll note that some use the exact same question for each course or grade level, and in others, they use a variation of the same question.

Middle School Vertical Social Studies Team

In this situation, this middle school social studies team is assessing the same learning target and using the same questions, but each grade level will use a different piece of stimulus information on their assessment. These teachers are all teaching the standard, "Cite specific textual evidence to support analysis of primary and secondary sources" (RH.6–8.1). In this case, the team decides to address the first target: "Cite specific text evidence to support analysis of primary source documents" in the instructional unit for November. Team members agree that during this unit, they will focus on written primary-source documents. Teachers choose an appropriate written document related to the content of the course they teach: ancient Egypt in sixth grade, the Revolutionary War in seventh grade, and the Constitution in eighth grade.

They build their assessment around the same two questions:

1. In class, we studied how historians analyze primary-source documents to understand more about what was happening during the time period the document was created. Analyze this primary-source document by making at least three inferences about time, place, audience, or events and support your inference with evidence from the text.

2. What is a question the author left unanswered, and what evidence supports this?

The stimulus primary-source documents connect to the content of each course and are appropriate for that grade level. When team members discuss this assessment, they naturally talk about how they teach their students to read primary-source documents and what their expectations for proficiency are. They come to agreement on what they expect from students' answers to their questions and build a common rubric they can use to score responses from each grade level. See figure 8.1 for an example of what such a rubric might look like.

Learning Target	Beyond Proficiency	Proficiency	Partial Proficiency	No Proficiency
The student can cite specific text evidence to support analysis of primary sources.	The student can analyze a primary-source document by making correct inferences and connections to historical facts. The student can support this analysis with evidence from the document. In addition, the student can also identify facts that have historical significance and places where the author leaves the analysis uncertain.	The student can analyze a primary-source document by making correct inferences and connections to historical facts. The student can support that analysis with evidence from the source.	The student can make some accurate inferences from primary sources but can't fully analyze the text and cite evidence to support that analysis.	The answer is incomplete or incorrect.

Figure 8.1: Sample common rubric across grade levels.

Middle School Vertical Mathematics Team

In another example, let's look at a middle school mathematics team who will assess a skill that each member is teaching and assessing but will use different questions on their assessments. It decides to focus on creating a common formative assessment for Mathematical Practice 3: "Construct viable arguments and critique the reasoning of others" (NGA & CCSSO, 2010b). The team decides to specifically focus on the learning target "Justify why an answer makes sense or is reasonable" (Kanold-McIntyre, Larson, & Briars, 2015). In this case, the students will receive realistic problems connected to the grade-level content, but teachers will ask them to justify why an answer makes sense or is reasonable. The team establishes its expectations for how students can justify why an answer makes sense or is unreasonable. Prior to choosing the problems for the assessment, the team discusses the fact that it wants students to be able to do more than find calculation errors, and members make sure that the problems used will require students to do that. They develop a rubric (see figure 8.2) to use whenever they are assessing this mathematics practice.

The sixth-grade team uses a problem that asks the following question: Micah constructs a rectangular prism with a volume of 360 cubic units. The height of the prism is 10 units. Micah claims that the base of the prism must be a square. Draw one sample prism that shows Micah is not correct in his thinking (SBAC, n.d.c).

Learning Target	Beyond Proficiency	Proficiency	Partial Proficiency	No Proficiency
Justify why an answer makes sense or is reasonable.	The student correctly evaluates the conclusion, provides full support of his or her reasoning, and extends the answer to include generalizations to other examples of where this is true.	The student correctly evaluates the conclusion by critiquing the chosen solution pathway, evaluating the mathematical reasoning, and correctly fixing calculation errors.	The student correctly evaluates only one or two parts of the conclusion: the solution pathway, the mathematical reasoning, or fixing calculation errors.	The answer is inaccurate or incomplete.

Figure 8.2: Sample common rubric for assessing similar skills in mathematics.

The seventh-grade teacher uses the following problem: Consider the inequality $5x < 50$. Jason says that any value for x that is less than 15 makes the inequality true. Provide at least one specific example to show that Jason is incorrect and explain why this is so.

The eighth-grade teacher uses the following question:

> Kyle was given the following problem to solve. A company sells baseball gloves and bats. The baseball gloves regularly cost $30 and the bats regularly cost $90. The gloves are on sale for $4 off, and the bats are on sale for 10% off. The goal is to sell $1200 worth of bats and gloves each week. Last week the store sold 14 gloves and 9 bats. Did the store meet its goal? The steps that Kyle used to solve the problem are shown. (M-STEP, n.d.)

There are five steps listed, and students are asked to choose the first step that has an error and explain what Kyle should have done instead (SBAC, 2015c).

High School Vertical Science Team

Finally, consider a high school science team comprising one earth science teacher, one biology teacher, and one chemistry and physics teacher. They start by each choosing the essential standards for their courses and find that they've all chosen a particular sequence of science standards as essential.

- **High school earth and space science:** Plan and conduct an investigation of the properties of water and its effects on Earth materials and surface processes (HS-ESS2-5; NGSS Lead States, 2013).

- **High school biology:** Plan and conduct an investigation to provide evidence that feedback mechanisms maintain homeostasis (HI-LS1-3; NGSS Lead States, 2013).

- **High school chemistry:** Plan and conduct an investigation to provide evidence that the transfer of thermal energy when two components of different temperature are combined within a closed system results in a more uniform energy distribution among the components in the system (second law of thermodynamics) (HS-PS3-4; NGSS Lead States, 2013).

- **High school physics:** Plan and conduct an investigation to provide evidence that an electric current can produce a magnetic field and that a changing magnetic field can produce an electric current (HS-PS2-5; NGSS Lead States, 2013).

In this case, the team discusses and decides that these standards are essential in every one of these courses. The team members work together to plan the common formative assessment, which will have the same or similar questions, but the science concept students will investigate will differ for each course. They agree that they want to focus on the target asking students to plan an investigation during this first assessment. They want students to make a strong hypothesis and acceptable predictions about what the results will be. Team members discuss what the criteria are for a strong hypothesis and what they would expect the predictions to look like. They create examples that fit their criteria and discuss what incorrect answers they might expect. The team then uses these decisions to write and score assessments on planning an investigation.

Assess by Learning Progression

The second way a vertical team can approach a common assessment is to build a rubric based on the progression from one grade level (or content area to another). We share examples of teams doing this work in the following sections.

Secondary Vertical English Language Arts Team

A small secondary English language arts team is working to determine the progression from sixth grade through twelfth grade for the learning target "Assess the reasoning and evidence from an argument text." See figure 8.3.

In this case, the team has determined, using the Common Core ELA standards (NGA & CCSSO, 2010a), how students' thinking should progress each year. They've looked across grade levels at the eighth Reading Standard for Informational Text, and followed one learning target from that standard (how an author supports a strong argument) as it is built on in middle and high school.

Learning Target	Eleventh–Twelfth-Grade Proficiency	Ninth–Tenth-Grade Proficiency	Eighth-Grade Proficiency	Seventh-Grade Proficiency	Sixth-Grade Proficiency
Assess the reasoning and evidence from an argument text.	Student is able to assess reasoning and evidence from seminal texts, including the constitutional principle and use of legal reasoning and the premises, purposes, and arguments in works of public advocacy.	Student is able to assess whether the reasoning is valid and the evidence is relevant and sufficient. Student can identify false claims in fallacious reasoning.	Student is able to determine if the support provided is sound and if the reasoning is specific, identifying what is irrelevant.	Student is able to distinguish claims that are effectively supported by sound reasoning and relevant and sufficient evidence.	Student is able to distinguish claims that are effectively supported by reasons and evidence.

Figure 8.3: Learning progression from sixth grade through twelfth grade.

The common formative assessment that the team uses may ask the student to analyze the reasoning and evidence from an argument text but will expect the student to provide a more nuanced analysis as he or she moves through the progression. Additionally, the text stimulus each teacher uses is different so that reading-level expectations will fit the grade the students are in.

When developing the assessment, the team members analyze each text to see what they believe a proficient student should be able to conclude as he or she evaluates the argument and reasoning. When using a rubric with a progression such as this one, a student can also see what demonstration of the *beyond proficiency* level would look like. For example, an eighth-grade student could demonstrate that he or she is beyond proficient by looking for false claims and fallacious reasoning because that performance level isn't an expectation until grades 9–10.

Elementary Vertical Team

Let's explore what a team assessing skills built as a progression with increasing complexity from one grade to the next could look like in a small elementary school with only one teacher teaching each grade level. Third-grade teacher Ann Butler is the team leader and begins the meeting with a quick review of norms, emphasizing the norm that everyone will contribute to the discussion since they have been having some difficulty following this norm in the last several meetings. Ann reminds the team members of the following grade-level standards they examined in a previous meeting:

> Determine the main idea of a text; recount the key details and explain how they support the main idea. (RI.3.2)
>
> Determine the main idea of a text and explain how it is supported by key details; summarize the text. (RI.4.2)
>
> Determine two or more main ideas of a text and explain how they are supported by key details; summarize the text. (RI.5.2)

She notes that, during their earlier discussion, they noticed that in grades 3 and 4, students would work with a text having one main idea versus two or more main ideas in grade 5. They also saw that students must be able to give a summary of a text in both fourth and fifth grade. At the time, they discussed their expectations for a summary at each of these grades so that the fifth-grade teacher would increase the expectations of proficiency from those of fourth graders. As they worked to build consensus, they decided to keep this standard as essential for third and fifth graders. They remembered that during their discussion of essential standards, they decided that they wanted the third-grade teacher to make sure those students were able to read a text and pick out its main idea and also be able to identify which details the author uses to support it. The fourth-grade standard was similar, with the addition of writing a summary. They decided that they wanted to wait until fifth grade to make this an essential standard because students will come to fifth grade knowing some ideas about how to write a summary. The fifth-grade team decided to add to their standard that students understand the summary should *not* include their personal views. Now they are ready to write the common formative assessment for grades 3 and 5. The team must decide at this point whether all three teachers will continue to work together to ensure the fourth-grade teacher will thoroughly understand what incoming students will know, or if the third- and fifth-grade teachers will develop and use the assessment in their partnership only. Because the team has recently felt less cohesive in their work on assessments, team members agree that they will all work together in developing this assessment.

Ann facilitates the discussion about which targets to assess. They decide on two learning targets for each grade: "Determine the main idea of the text and explain how the key details support the main idea" for third grade, and "Determine two or more main ideas of a text and summarize the text" for fifth grade. Ann then asks the team for thoughts about the stimulus text. Jeremy, the fifth-grade teacher, suggests that it will be important to use different texts for each grade level since the expectation for choosing one main idea in third grade and multiple main ideas in fifth grade will require texts of increasing complexity. They recognize that finding an appropriate text is often the hardest part of writing English language arts assessments and know that the three of them working together will likely be more successful than any of them working in isolation. Sarah Carter, the fourth-grade teacher, suggests that they look on the Smithsonian TweenTribune website (http://tweentribune.com) to find one article suited to third grade and a second article suited to fifth grade, both of which they can use to see if students can identify the main idea and details that support it.

Once they find their texts, the questions are easy to write. Ann facilitates the discussion, and all three teachers make suggestions about appropriate wording. For the first target in third grade, they will start with a constructed-response question that asks for the main idea of the text. For fifth grade, they revise the question to ask the student to identify two or more main ideas of the text. For the second learning target, Sarah believes that the questions will be different because the targets are different. She recommends that they ask third graders to explain how the key details support the main idea and ask fifth graders to summarize the text. Ann reminds them that it is important to discuss and clarify what acceptable answers will look like, as well as predict possible wrong answers. During this discussion, all three teachers clarify for themselves what it looks like to move from third to fourth to fifth grade. They also discuss what the fourth-grade teacher will expect in a summary that is different for what the fifth-grade teacher will expect. Together they develop the following rubric, provided in figure 8.4.

Grade Level and Learning Target	Beyond Proficiency	Proficiency	Partial Proficiency	No Proficiency
3—Explain how the key details support the main idea.	There is no beyond proficiency for this target.	The student accurately identifies and cites key details that support the main idea and is able to explain how the details connect to the main idea.	The student accurately identifies and cites the key details that support the main idea but is not able to explain how these details connect to the main idea.	The answer is incomplete or inaccurate.
4—Summarize the text.	There is no beyond proficiency for this target.	The summary includes all relevant points (includes the main idea, includes the specific details from the text that support the main idea, uses sequential order, avoids personal opinion or unrelated details, is shorter than the text).	The summary includes some but not all of the relevant points.	The answer is incomplete or inaccurate.
5—Summarize the text.	There is no beyond proficiency for this target.	The summary includes all relevant points (includes the main idea, includes the specific details from the text that support the main idea, uses sequential order, avoids personal opinion or unrelated details, is shorter than the text).	The summary includes some but not all of the relevant points.	The answer is incomplete or inaccurate.

Figure 8.4: Third- through fifth-grade rubric.

Sarah wants to include the expectations for fourth grade even though her students aren't participating in the common formative assessment. She believes it's important that students understand what the expectations will be for these targets. The third- and fifth-grade teachers administer the assessment, and then the entire team comes back together to discuss the results.

You might notice in the rubric that the team decided that there is no beyond proficiency for this target. In chapter 5, we discussed the fact that some learning targets don't have a beyond proficiency level. This target is one that fits this criteria. Some teams might make the beyond proficiency designation the next grade-level target, but we discourage this as it is acceleration rather than differentiation.

Interdisciplinary Teams

Another common way for singleton teachers to configure their teams is an interdisciplinary structure in which teachers share students but not content. We share examples of these types of teams working together to write assessments in the following sections.

Eighth-Grade Interdisciplinary Team

This eighth-grade middle school interdisciplinary team consists of an English language arts teacher, a mathematics teacher, a science teacher, and a social studies teacher. Notice that in this example, only two of the team members work on a common assessment because they are the only teachers on the team who identify matching essential learning targets on this topic. For an upcoming common assessment, the English language arts teacher and the science teacher want to assess their students' abilities to support claims in writing with logical reasoning and relevant evidence for the ELA class and support claims with accurate data and evidence for the science class (NGA & CCSSO, 2010a). During instruction, each of these teachers works on the specific targets for his or her content area: the English teacher focuses on logical reasoning and relevant evidence; the science teacher works on how to use data tables to support the claim being made. For their common formative assessment, team members decide to give one assessment based on an article about the biochemical evidence for evolution. This text includes written information along with data tables to support the claims. The team asks students to write a piece of text in which they develop a claim about whether two animals are related by a common ancestor. The teachers direct students to use the facts from the text as well as the data from the tables in the article to support their claims. They create a rubric that includes both learning targets: (1) using logical reasons and relevant evidence and (2) using data analysis to support the claim.

Ninth-Grade Interdisciplinary Team

In another example, a team in a very small high school with only one mathematics, science, social studies, and English language arts teacher might work together on one of their learning targets related to critical thinking for their ninth-grade students: "Evaluate the quality of proposed solutions to real-life, realistic problems and suggest alternative solutions that will likely work if an aspect of the problem were to change." The English language arts teacher and the social studies teacher choose a piece of text about the history of gun control legislation over the last five decades in which the author looks at how rules about applying for a permit have changed as well as how the types of items citizens can own have changed. Students must choose one of these measures and evaluate the quality of evidence the author has provided. Teachers then ask them to consider how the advance of 3-D printers that can make plastic guns, which cannot be identified by metal detectors, affects the solution the text offers.

At the same time, the mathematics teacher addresses the same target, providing students with a problem from a manufacturer who wants to make cardboard boxes with the least amount of waste possible. The problem tells students the volume of the content that needs to ship and gives three different sets of dimensions for boxes, then asks them to determine which set will be both able to ship the items and the least costly. They must explain how they arrived at their decision. Then they determine the least costly dimensions for a box that would ship a different volume of material.

Cross-School and District Teams

Teams of teachers who work across schools and districts are most frequently organized around the common course or grade they teach. For example, a district may have two high schools that each have a physics teacher. These two teachers will develop and use common assessments the same way a team who works in the same building works. They start by agreeing on the essential standards and build pacing guides to determine when they will teach and address each of the essential learning targets. When writing their common formative assessments, they will work either in person or electronically to write the questions and establish the answer key.

Electronic Teams

Most often, an electronic team operates the same way a team that shares the same course or content does. The only difference is that the members aren't in the same room when they are having their meetings but, rather, rely on electronic communication (such as Google Hangouts or Skype) to meet in a virtual environment. In these cases, the steps of developing and using common assessments are the same as those described in previous chapters.

Analyzing Data in Teams Configured Around Singleton Teachers

We need to recognize that when teams use common formative assessments in these structures, they may need to tweak the protocols and processes that traditionally structured teams use since they likely have different stimuli or, in the case of interdisciplinary teams, different content. However, the goal still remains the same: knowing what students have learned, student by student and target by target. We have some suggestions about how to start this process, but these are only a starting point, not an ending point. Every team will find, as we have in working with colleagues doing this work, that there may be steps that are out of order for the way it works, questions that it must add or tweak, and processes that either don't fit or require modification.

We do, however, recommend that all teams follow a protocol during data meetings. A protocol helps teams stay on task, avoid pitfalls and speed bumps, handle conversations that may be a bit awkward, and get to the best answers about how to help students. To get started, we recommend the team chooses one of the two protocols we've offered in chapter 6: Protocol for Using Common Summative Assessment Data (table 6.1, page 81) or Protocol for Using Common Formative Assessment Data (table 6.2, page 82), depending on which type of assessment they've written. Visit **go.SolutionTree.com/assessment** for free reproducible versions of these tables. Next, we'll explore two sample scenarios that feature teams analyzing data from their common assessments.

Middle School Vertical Social Studies Team

The vertical social studies team (for sixth, seventh, and eighth grade) at Nirvana Middle School has given a common formative assessment that assessed a common skill related to primary-source documents. Let's explore a little deeper what might happen at the data meeting when the three social studies teachers from the middle school vertical social studies team introduced earlier in this chapter get together to analyze the results of the common formative assessment they developed. The team is assessing the learning target "Cite text evidence to support the analysis of primary-source documents." When this team wrote its common formative assessment, each grade-level teacher found a primary-source document (in this case, a piece of text) that connected to the content they are currently teaching. The team settled on two constructed-response questions that would be identical for each grade.

1. In class, we studied how historians analyze primary-source documents to understand more about what was happening during the time period the document was created. Analyze this primary-source document by making at least three inferences about time, place, audience, or events, and support each inference with evidence from the text.

2. What is one question the author left unanswered? What evidence did the author provide, and what evidence is missing about that question?

Before they administer the common formative assessment, the team members agree on what the possible correct answers would be for each grade and develop a common rubric for assessing student responses.

After administering the common formative assessment, the team gathers to analyze the data, using the Protocol for Using Common Formative Assessment Data (table 6.2, page 82). Team members begin their meeting with step 1 as they review the purpose of the meeting and their data norms. During step 2, team members review the learning target and the proficiency expectations, reminding each other that the students must have scored at the proficiency level on the rubric for question 1, and that question 2 is only considered for those who were proficient on question 1, as it indicates whether the student is beyond proficient. Using step 3, they then focus on the first learning target, which asks students to analyze a primary-source document to make and support inferences about time, place, audience, and events. Each of the teachers shares the numbers of students who were proficient and who were not. They also determine how many students who were proficient also got question 2 correct. During step 4, they use the pile and plan method of analyzing data (see chapter 6). Each teacher creates two piles (correct and incorrect answers) and begins to examine the incorrect answers and discuss his or her students' misunderstandings or mistakes when answering the first question. As they look through the student responses, they see that most of the students could identify the place and the events that were occurring. Because the documents were tightly connected to the time period and events they were currently studying, the team felt there were fairly easy inferences to make. But since they had asked for at least three inferences, students had to address at least one more part of the question. Regarding time, they found that many students were able to accurately identify when the text was written, but some couldn't support their answer from the text. The team creates a separate pile for the group of students who missed most of the clues associated with the correct time period. What the team found intriguing was that the seventh-grade text was a memoir that a Civil War soldier wrote well after the Civil War. This time disconnect confused some students about when it was written. The team spends some time talking about how to best address the misconception for this group, even though it is only the seventh-grade teacher who needs to respond to this misconception. The members know that they can come up with a better response together than individually. They also see that many students had difficulty identifying the audience of the source. As they identify each misunderstanding or misconception, they plan a corrective instruction strategy to overcome the problem.

The team also has a group of students who accurately answered the second question, which was included to identify students who could already go beyond proficiency for the learning target on the assessment. For these students, the team decides to challenge them by giving them some historical political cartoons and asking them to work in small groups to design a political cartoon that could be effective in reflecting current politics in the United States. After they finish planning the response, they decide how they would reassess those who weren't proficient. The team decides to use another primary-source document and focus on only the first question.

Elementary School Vertical Grades 3–5 Team

This team decides to develop a common formative assessment for learning targets that come from standard 3 for the CCSS strand Reading Informational Text in each grade level (RI.3.3, RI.4.3, and RI.5.3; NGA & CCSSO, 2010a) and use a learning progression. This vertical team configuration includes one third-grade teacher, one fourth-grade teacher, and one fifth-grade teacher. The third-grade learning target is, "Students can describe the relationship between science concepts in a text, using language that pertains to cause and effect." The fourth-grade learning target is, "Students can explain concepts in a scientific text supported by information from the text." The fifth-grade learning target is, "Students can explain the relationships or interactions of two concepts in a scientific text based on information from the text."

The team decides to use an online article about how ecosystems are changing due to global warming. Using a website (such as http://newsela.com) that provides current event articles that can be downloaded at different Lexile levels, the team members choose one text at the third-grade level and a second text written at the fourth- and fifth-grade level.

In this case, the constructed-response questions are different for each grade level because they want to assess the specific learning target for that grade. The item for third graders is, "The author of this article explains how global warming causes some animals to change where they are living. Explain why this is happening using details you learned from the text." The fourth graders see, "The author of this article explains why some animals are found in different oceans and on different continents than before. Explain why scientists think this is happening using specific details from the text." The fifth graders get, "In this article, the author explains the scientific term *faunal exchange* and describes how animals are found in different oceans and on different continents than before. Use details from the text to describe why scientists believe this has occurred and what they predict might happen in the future." While each teacher has a slightly different version of the common formative assessment (different question or different Lexile level of text), the assessment is similar enough to make the data analysis effective.

At the data meeting, each teacher brings his or her students' work to the table. After reviewing the learning targets and expectation for proficiency (3 out of 4 on the rubric for each grade level), they use the pile and plan method to analyze the mistakes in the students' answers and to determine how many students will need corrective instruction. The third-grade teacher has two students who weren't able to use details from the text in their answers. The fourth-grade teacher has three students who couldn't answer the question correctly, but the fifth-grade teacher has ten students who had difficulty with their question. After some discussion about the students' misunderstandings and misconceptions, the team determines that the students in third and fourth grade who were not proficient all missed the cues from the headings in the text. The team decides to group all five of these students together (across grade levels) since they all need similar corrective instruction. Meanwhile, they will keep the fifth-grade students together who need help and will focus on strategies to use with difficult vocabulary. For the students who were proficient at each grade level, they decide to each keep their own students and give them a different scientific text (written at their grade level) with the text features removed. They will ask students to work in cooperative groups to develop examples of text features that would help the reader understand the text.

Conclusion

While it can be challenging for singletons to collaborate, team structures including vertical teams, interdisciplinary teams, cross-school and district teams, and electronic teams make the work of creating and using common formative assessments possible in their varied settings. By being creative, collaborative teams who don't share the exact same content can develop and use common formative assessments to help determine how to best help their students. When team members believe they can work better together than in isolation, they can effectively use formative assessments that may not be exactly alike.

TIPS FOR TRACTION

- There are four typical configurations for singleton teams: vertical teams, interdisciplinary teams, cross-school and district teams, and electronic teams.

- Team members in these teams still write common formative assessments around essential learning targets; not every team member has to participate in every common formative assessment.

- Some teams comprising multiple grade levels vary the stimulus used in their assessments and keep the same question; others use different questions for each grade level.

EPILOGUE

Writing and using common assessments can be challenging work. However, common assessments can fuel the work of professional learning communities and drive improvements in their students' achievement. It is our hope that this book has met our goal to empower teams in this challenging work by simplifying the process and providing a clear path to help teams get started.

That said, however, we know that no single book or strategy should be considered as the only way to approach this work. We encourage teams to take these ideas and make them work for your team and your students—don't be limited only by what we've shared here, but use the information as a starting point. The power of collaboration ensures that you will be better as a result of the interactions with other teachers who care as deeply as you do about your students. We know that each collaborative team brings its own expertise to the table when developing assessments and using the results. Because of this, we know that no book can ever make the process easy for teachers to complete. However, our goal with this book was to take what we've learned from the schools and districts we've worked with and develop a streamlined process that teams can follow to make this complex process a little simpler.

Writing and using common assessments are about learning together how to better support students in becoming college and career ready as they leave high school. Just as one book can't make the process easy, one teacher can't provide all the necessary support for every student. High-performing teams trust each other and work collaboratively to provide the very best for each student.

Finally, we know that when assessments are designed well they provide very specific information for teams to use in planning their responses. Most every school we've worked with has had an experience trying to respond to data from a poorly constructed assessment. We believe that the strategies we're suggesting for planning and writing quality assessments will make the data analysis simpler and more effective. We hope that, as you develop confidence in your own assessment skills, you will become more excited about this process and how it will impact your instruction.

Using a Road Map to Implement Common Assessments

One thing we know about the collaborative teams that create common assessments is that no one wants to scrap all the hard work he or she has already done. That's why we decided to include what we call a road map for assessments in this book. We designed the road map in five parts, based on the order that makes most sense for doing this work: (1) understanding the role of essential standards; (2) aligning curriculum, instruction, and assessments; (3) developing quality formative assessments; (4) using data from assessments; and (5) involving students in the process. We present each part in rubric form for teams to assess their current state and work toward improvement. There are four stages of implementation for each item: (1) pre-initiating, (2) initiating, (3) developing, and (4) sustaining (DuFour et al., 2016). We know that many teams will be at more advanced stages in some sections than in others. As teams use this map, they may find that they've successfully implemented steps in some sections but not in others. We recommend that teams start by highlighting the stage they've reached for each of the steps that they've successfully implemented. For example, let's say that a team is at the developing stage for identifying essential standards but only at the initiating stage for unwrapping the standards. The next step is to move ahead to the developing stage on unwrapping the essential standards in common formative assessments. Once teams identify the stage they've reached, the road map lists the chapter in this book where they can find their next steps.

Finally, we encourage teams *not* to use this as a checklist of things to do but rather as a way to continually improve their work to help all students learn at high levels. Teams will find that, as they gain more experience, the assessments they write improve and the planned responses do as well. Consider this process a journey that will lead to some interesting and complex places, but one that never is complete. Continual improvement is the ultimate goal. See figures A.1 through A.5 (pages 124–128).

	Stage 1: Pre-Initiating	Stage 2: Initiating	Stage 3: Developing	Stage 4: Sustaining
Identifying essential standards (See chapter 2, page 17.)	We haven't yet, as a collaborative team, identified the essential standards either unit by unit or for the entire year.	We know what essential standards are and have discussed how we will complete the process.	We have identified the essential standards and have vertically aligned them for our course or grade level.	We have identified our essential standards and communicated them to other teams, students, and parents.
Getting clear on the standards: The unwrapping process (See chapter 2, page 17.)	We haven't yet started identifying the learning targets that we will use in our work.	We've started the process of identifying learning targets by looking at the key words in the standards (nouns, verbs, context).	We have unwrapped each of our standards to determine both explicit and implicit learning targets that we must teach and assess, including the academic vocabulary. We have also discussed the rigor of each of the targets, using a common language such as DOK.	Each collaborative team understands how the learning targets teachers are teaching fit vertically with the grade level or course before theirs and the grade level or course after theirs.
Understanding the expectations for rigor (See chapter 3, page 33.)	We haven't yet built an understanding of the expectations for rigor that we must use in our instruction and assessments.	We have begun the discussions about what rigor should look like and are learning more about DOK and the tasks associated with each level. We are learning how to develop tasks at a variety of DOK levels.	We have begun designing instructional materials and tasks that mirror the expectations for rigor written in our standards. Additionally, we have investigated learning progressions to plan scaffolded strategies to help students learn more rigorous targets.	We have aligned the assessments we use to the anticipated rigor we want our students to master.

Figure A.1: Understanding the role of essential standards.

Visit go.SolutionTree.com/assessment for a free reproducible version of this figure.

	Stage 1: Pre-Initiating	Stage 2: Initiating	Stage 3: Developing	Stage 4: Sustaining
Identifying units of study (See chapter 4, page 51.)	We haven't developed units of instruction that include all of the standards we are expected to teach.	We are working together to make sure that we align all of our units of instruction to the standards. As we identify gaps and redundancies, we are comfortable changing the curriculum or removing unnecessary units to align to the standards.	Our curriculum units are totally aligned to our standards. We have assigned all learning targets to one or more units. The units we've developed reflect the emphasis for our essential standards.	We evaluate the effectiveness of our curriculum by examining the results of our summative assessments and especially the end-of-year tests. We discuss whether we need to change the curriculum based on our student achievement results.

	Stage 1: Pre-Initiating	Stage 2: Initiating	Stage 3: Developing	Stage 4: Sustaining
Creating pacing guides (See chapter 4, page 51.)	We haven't yet created pacing guides that reflect consensus on how much time we should dedicate to each unit or standard.	We are in the process of developing pacing guides that reflect consensus among team members about how much time we need for students to learn the essential standards in each unit.	We use our pacing guides effectively and are able to give common formative assessments together, discuss the results, and develop corrective instruction efficiently and effectively.	We modify our pacing guides whenever we see a reason to do so. We know that, over time, our students will come better prepared to learn the essential standards for our grade level or course, and this will require us to change our pacing.
Aligning instructional and assessment strategies (See chapter 4, page 51.)	We haven't yet started to examine the alignment among our curriculum, instruction, and assessments.	We have begun to work collaboratively to identify the instructional strategies aligned to our proficiency expectations. As a team, we value learning together about these strategies.	We have changed our instructional strategies to ensure we're using best practices to help students reach proficiency. We understand that more rigorous curriculum requires different strategies.	We continue to evaluate the effectiveness of the strategies we're using by examining the results of all of our assessments. We compare the results of one strategy against another and value the information we get back.
Determining when to give common formative assessments (See chapter 4, page 51.)	We haven't yet identified when we will use common formative assessments in our work.	We have examined our units of instruction to see where we teach the essential standards. We plan to write common formative assessments approximately once every three weeks.	In addition to the common formative assessments we developed during our first year of implementation, we have added additional assessments (common formative as well as common summative) around our essential standards.	We are always looking for ways to improve the frequency and effectiveness of assessment.

Figure A.2: Aligning curriculum, instruction, and assessments.

Visit **go.SolutionTree.com/assessment** *for a free reproducible version of this figure.*

	Stage 1: Pre-Initiating	Stage 2: Initiating	Stage 3: Developing	Stage 4: Sustaining
Creating an assessment plan (See chapter 5, page 61.)	We don't use assessment plans to guide our assessment work.	We're learning about planning our assessments prior to writing them. We know that this is important to creating a valid assessment.	For each assessment we write, we list the targets to assess and match them to the type of items we will use. We also plan how many questions we will link to each target.	We continually evaluate the effectiveness of each assessment plan after we give the assessment to determine if we assessed the right targets and chose the best item type.

Figure A.3: Developing quality common formative assessments.

continued →

	Stage 1: Pre-Initiating	Stage 2: Initiating	Stage 3: Developing	Stage 4: Sustaining
Writing quality questions (See chapter 5, page 61.)	We haven't yet started to look at the issues connected with writing quality questions.	We are learning about writing quality questions and are applying it to our work. We know that with practice we will become better at this process and continue to learn by doing.	We make sure our questions are clear to students, lay out expectations for what we want students to include in the answer, and don't include words or ideas intended to trick students.	We continually evaluate the alignment and effectiveness of assessments (for example, using the ACID [aligned, clearly written, informative, designed] test) to determine if we assessed the right targets and chose or designed the best item types. If not, we develop better questions and save them for the next time we assess that learning target.
Developing the answer key or rubrics (See chapter 5, page 61.)	We don't use answer keys or rubrics in our assessment work.	We are starting to write answer keys for our assessments with at least the correct responses included. We are writing rubrics for our team to use in scoring student responses but haven't yet put them in student-friendly language.	We develop answer keys while we are writing our assessments. They include both correct and possible incorrect responses. We agree on how many questions students have to answer correctly to be proficient. We include rubrics for constructed-response questions and write them in student-friendly language.	We evaluate both our answer keys and our rubrics after each assessment. We have practiced collaborative scoring frequently so that we know we are scoring assessments the same way.

*Visit **go.SolutionTree.com/assessment** for a free reproducible version of this figure.*

	Stage 1: Pre-Initiating	Stage 2: Initiating	Stage 3: Developing	Stage 4: Sustaining
Using the correct data for the purpose (See chapter 6, page 77.)	We haven't yet explored whether the assessments we're using match their purpose.	We have started identifying the purpose of each assessment before we use it. We are learning about wide-angle and close-up questions so that we carefully choose the assessments we use.	We are using a variety of assessments confidently as we match the assessment type to our purposes.	We have evaluated the variety of assessments we use and have eliminated those that are redundant and added those that we still needed.

	Stage 1: Pre-Initiating	Stage 2: Initiating	Stage 3: Developing	Stage 4: Sustaining
Using protocols for data discussions (See chapter 6, page 77.)	We haven't yet developed and used protocols in our assessment work.	We understand why protocols are necessary to keep our data discussions focused and on track. We've started to use them but aren't yet comfortable with the process.	We use different protocols in our data discussions, depending on what type of assessment data we have. We are confident that we are able to navigate complex issues without getting sidetracked.	We evaluate the effectiveness of our data discussions. We look at both efficiency and effectiveness and discuss how to improve both.
Developing an effective response (See chapter 6, page 77.)	Our responses to assessments are not always effective.	We are learning how to develop our responses to common formative assessments student by student and learning target by learning target. We are also using our summative assessments more effectively to evaluate our SMART goals, identify students who urgently need help, and evaluate our pacing guides and curriculum units.	We are confident that we can effectively use both common summative and common formative assessments to plan corrective instruction and intervention. We design these responses based on the results from specific assessments.	We evaluate the effectiveness of our responses to both summative and formative assessments. We are comfortable changing our practices when the evidence shows us we need to.

Figure A.4: Using data from assessments.

*Visit **go.SolutionTree.com/assessment** for a free reproducible version of this figure.*

	Stage 1: Pre-Initiating	Stage 2: Initiating	Stage 3: Developing	Stage 4: Sustaining
Moving from using grades to using feedback (See chapter 7, page 93.)	We haven't yet examined our grading practices related to the assessment process.	We have agreed that we need to move away from grading formative assessments and, to that end, have started learning more about what makes quality feedback and how other teachers have taken this step.	We have begun to use descriptive feedback on our formative assessments. We are helping students see its purpose and how they should respond to their own feedback. We have seen the language we're using change from grades to scores.	Students seek feedback from teachers as well as peers. They understand and value the purpose of knowing the learning targets, of formative assessment, and of feedback.

Figure A.5: Involving students in the process.

continued →

	Stage 1: Pre-Initiating	Stage 2: Initiating	Stage 3: Developing	Stage 4: Sustaining
Building a learning partnership with students (See chapter 7, page 93.)	We haven't yet explored how to involve students in the assessment process.	Our students are building a growth mindset and know what expected targets of learning are for each lesson.	Students see formative assessment as evidence they can use to know what they've learned as well as what they still need to learn.	Student learning is an equal partnership between the teacher and student. Students fully understand what proficiency looks like and are engaged in getting to that point and beyond.

*Visit **go.SolutionTree.com/assessment** for a free reproducible version of this figure.*

REFERENCES AND RESOURCES

Ainsworth, L. (2010). *Rigorous curriculum design: How to create curricular units of study that align standards, instruction, and assessment.* Englewood, CO: Lead + Learn Press.

Ainsworth, L. (2013). *Prioritizing the Common Core: Identifying the specific standards to emphasize the most.* Englewood, CO: Lead + Learn Press.

American Institutes for Research. (2013, August 26). *Smarter Balanced Assessment Consortium: Practice test scoring guide—Grade 4 performance task.* Accessed at www.smarterbalanced.org/wp-content /uploads/2015/11/G4_Practice_Test_Scoring_Guide_Math_PT.pdf on April 4, 2016.

Aungst, G. (2014). Using Webb's Depth of Knowledge to increase rigor. *Edutopia.* Accessed at www .edutopia.org/blog/webbs-depth-knowledge-increase-rigor-gerald-aungst on September 2, 2016.

Bailey, K., & Jakicic, C. (2012). *Common formative assessment: A toolkit for Professional Learning Communities at Work.* Bloomington, IN: Solution Tree Press.

Bailey, K., Jakicic, C., & Spiller, J. (2014). *Collaborating for success with the Common Core: A toolkit for Professional Learning Communities at Work.* Bloomington, IN: Solution Tree Press.

Bangert-Drowns, R. L., Kulik, J. A., & Kulik, C.-L. C. (1991). Effects of frequent classroom testing. *Journal of Educational Research, 85*(2), 89–99.

Black, P., & Wiliam, D. (1998). Inside the black box: Raising standards through classroom assessment. *Phi Delta Kappan, 80*(2), 139–148.

Briars, D. J., Asturias, H., Foster, D., & Gale, M. A. (2013). *Common Core mathematics in a PLC at Work, grades 6–8.* T. D. Kanold (Ed.). Bloomington, IN: Solution Tree Press.

Brookhart, S. M. (2011). Starting the conversation about grading. *Educational Leadership, 69*(3), 10–14. Accessed at www.ascd.org/publications/educational-leadership/nov11/vol69/num03/Starting-the -Conversation-About-Grading.aspx on May 17, 2016.

Buffum, A., & Mattos, M. (Eds.). (2015). *It's about time: Planning interventions and extensions in elementary school.* Bloomington, IN: Solution Tree Press.

Buffum, A., Mattos, M., & Weber, C. (2012). *Simplifying response to intervention: Four essential guiding principles*. Bloomington, IN: Solution Tree Press.

Butler, R., & Nisan, M. (1986). Effects of no feedback, task-related comments, and grades on intrinsic motivation and performance. *Journal of Educational Psychology, 78*(3), 210–216.

California Department of Education. (2000, May). *History–social science content standards for California public schools: Kindergarten through grade twelve*. Sacramento: California Department of Education. Accessed at www.cde.ca.gov/be/st/ss/documents/histsocscistnd.pdf on April 4, 2016.

California Department of Education. (2009). *California standards test: Released test questions—Science grade 5*. Accessed at www.cde.ca.gov/ta/tg/sr/documents/cstrtqscience5.pdf on December 21, 2015.

Chappuis, S., Chappuis, J., & Stiggins, R. (2009). The quest for quality. *Educational Leadership, 67*(3), 14–19.

Charles A. Dana Center. (2016). *Classroom videos*. Accessed at www.insidemathematics.org/classroom-videos on August 5, 2015.

Consortium on Reaching Excellence in Education. (2013). *Problem solving in elementary math: Participant handout*. Berkeley, CA: Author. Accessed at www.corelearn.com/files/Problem%20Solving%20in%20Elem%20Math%20PRG_v2.1.pdf on April 4, 2016.

Conzemius, A. E., & O'Neill, J. (2014). *Handbook for SMART school teams* (2nd ed.). Bloomington, IN: Solution Tree Press.

Covey, S. R. (2012). *The 7 habits of highly effective people: Powerful lessons in personal change*. Salt Lake City, UT: FranklinCovey.

DuFour, R., DuFour, R., Eaker, R., & Many, T. W. (2010). *Learning by doing: A handbook for Professional Learning Communities at Work* (2nd ed.). Bloomington, IN: Solution Tree Press.

DuFour, R., DuFour, R., Eaker, R., Many, T. W., & Mattos, M. (2016). *Learning by doing: A handbook for Professional Learning Communities at Work* (3rd ed.). Bloomington, IN: Solution Tree Press.

DuFour, R., & Marzano, R. J. (2011). *Leaders of learning: How district, school, and classroom leaders improve student achievement*. Bloomington, IN: Solution Tree Press.

Dweck, C. S. (2008). *Mindset: The new psychology of success*. New York: Ballantine Books.

Dweck, C. S. (2014, December). *The power of believing that you can improve* [Video file]. Accessed at www.ted.com/talks/carol_dweck_the_power_of_believing_that_you_can_improve/transcript?language=en on April 4, 2016.

Ferriter, W. M. (2010, October 30). *Twitter for singletons in a PLC* [Blog post]. Accessed at www.teachingquality.org/content/blogs/bill-ferriter/twitter-singletons-plc on December 21, 2015.

Gareis, C. R., & Grant, L. W. (2008). *Teacher-made assessments: How to connect curriculum, instruction, and student learning*. Larchmont, NY: Eye on Education.

Guskey, T. R. (2015). *On your mark: Challenging the conventions of grading and reporting.* Bloomington, IN: Solution Tree Press.

Haladyna, T. M., & Downing, S. M. (1989). Validity of a taxonomy of multiple-choice item-writing rules. *Applied Measurement in Education, 2*(1), 51–78.

Hansen, A. (2015). *How to develop PLCs for singletons and small schools.* Bloomington, IN: Solution Tree Press.

Hattie, J. (1999, August 2). *Influences on student learning.* Accessed at http://projectlearning.org/blog /wp-content/uploads/2014/02/Influences-on-Student-Learning-John-Hattie.pdf on April 5, 2016.

Hattie, J. (2009). *Visible learning: A synthesis of over 800 meta-analyses relating to achievement.* New York: Routledge.

Hattie, J. (2012). *Visible learning for teachers: Maximizing impact on learning.* New York: Routledge.

Herman, J. L, & Linn, R. L. (2013, January). *On the road to assessing deeper learning: The status of Smarter Balanced and PARCC assessment consortia* (CRESST Report No. 823). Los Angeles: National Center for Research on Evaluation, Standards, and Student Testing. Accessed at www.cse.ucla .edu/products/reports/R823.pdf on April 5, 2016.

Hess, K. K. (2008). *Exploring cognitive demand in instruction and assessment.* Dover, NH: National Center for the Improvement of Educational Assessment. Accessed at www.nciea.org/publication _PDFs/DOK_ApplyingWebb_KH08.pdf on August 11, 2016.

Hess, K. K. (2013). *Linking research with practice: A local assessment toolkit to guide school leaders.* Dover, NH: National Center for the Improvement of Educational Assessment. Accessed at www.nciea .org/publication_PDFs/Linking_research_w_practice_module2_v2b%20KH022814.pdf on April 4, 2016.

Hess, K. K., Carlock, D., Jones, B., & Walkup, J. R. (2009*). What exactly do "fewer, clearer, and higher standards" really look like in the classroom? Using a cognitive rigor matrix to analyze curriculum, plan lessons, and implement assessments.* Underhill, VT: Educational Research in Action. Accessed at http://media.wix.com/ugd/5e86bd_2f72d4acd00a4494b0677adecafd119f.pdf on April 4, 2016.

Hess, K. K., & Hervey, S. (2010). Tools for examining text complexity. In K. K. Hess, *Linking research with practice: A local assessment toolkit to guide school leaders.* Dover, NH: National Center for the Improvement of Educational Assessment. Accessed at www.nciea.org/publication_PDFs /Linking_research_w_practice_module2_v2b%20KH022814.pdf on April 4, 2016.

Kanold-McIntyre, J., Larson, M. R., & Briars, D. J. (2015). *Beyond the Common Core: A handbook for mathematics in a PLC at Work, grades 6–8.* T. D. Kanold (Ed.). Bloomington, IN: Solution Tree Press.

Kildeer Countryside Community Consolidated School District 96. (n.d.). *Elementary pacing guides.* Accessed at www.kcsd96.org/curriculum/Elementary-Pacing-Guides.cfm on April 4, 2016.

Kopriva, R. (2008). What's wrong with wrong answers? *Harvard Education Letter, 24*(4), 6–8.

Lexile Framework for Reading. (2016). *Text complexity grade bands and Lexile bands.* Accessed at www .lexile.com/using-lexile/lexile-measures-and-the-ccssi/text-complexity-grade-bands-and-lexile -ranges on October 3, 2016.

Lipnevich, A. A., & Smith, J. K. (2008). Response to assessment feedback: The effects of grades, praise, and source of information. *ETS Research Report Series, 2008*(1), i-57.

Marzano, R. J. (2003). *What works in schools: Translating research into action.* Alexandria, VA: Association for Supervision and Curriculum Development.

Marzano, R. J. (2010). *Formative assessment and standards-based grading.* Bloomington, IN: Marzano Research.

Marzano, R. J., Pickering, D. J., & Pollock, J. E. (2001). *Classroom instruction that works: Research-based strategies for increasing student achievement.* Alexandria, VA: Association for Supervision and Curriculum Development.

Mattos, M., & Buffum, A. (Eds.). (2015). *It's about time: Planning interventions and extensions in secondary school.* Bloomington, IN: Solution Tree Press.

Mississippi Department of Education. (2009). *Webb's Depth of Knowledge guide: Career and technical education definitions* [Pamphlet]. Accessed at www.aps.edu/re/documents/resources/Webbs_DOK _Guide.pdf on April 4, 2016.

M-STEP Grade 8 Mathematics. (n.d.). *Sample.* Accessed at www.michigan.gov/documents/mde /Mathematics_Paper-Pencil_Sample_Item_Set-Grade_8_484491_7.pdf on October 3, 2016.

National Center for the Improvement of Educational Assessment. (n.d.). *Publications.* Accessed at www .nciea.org/cgi-bin/pubspage.cgi?sortby=pub_date on April 4, 2016.

National Governors Association Center for Best Practices & Council of Chief State School Officers. (n.d.a). *About the standards.* Accessed at www.corestandards.org/about-the-standards on April 4, 2016.

National Governors Association Center for Best Practices & Council of Chief State School Officers. (n.d.b). *Common Core State Standards for English language arts and literacy in history/social studies, science, and technical subjects: Appendix B—Text exemplars and sample performance tasks.* Washington, DC: Authors. Accessed at www.corestandards.org/assets/Appendix_B.pdf on April 4, 2016.

National Governors Association Center for Best Practices & Council of Chief State School Officers. (n.d.c). *Key shifts in English language arts.* Accessed at www.corestandards.org/other-resources /key-shifts-in-english-language-arts on April 4, 2016.

National Governors Association Center for Best Practices & Council of Chief State School Officers. (n.d.d). *Key shifts in mathematics.* Accessed at www.corestandards.org/other-resources/key-shifts -in-mathematics on April 4, 2016.

National Governors Association Center for Best Practices & Council of Chief State School Officers. (2010a). *Common Core State Standards for English language arts and literacy in history/social studies, science, and technical subjects.* Washington, DC: Authors. Accessed at www.corestandards.org /assets/CCSSI_ELA%20Standards.pdf on January 4, 2013.

National Governors Association Center for Best Practices & Council of Chief State School Officers. (2010b). *Common Core State Standards for mathematics.* Washington, DC: Authors. Accessed at www.corestandards.org/assets/CCSSI_Math%20Standards.pdf on January 4, 2013.

NGSS Lead States. (2013). *Next Generation Science Standards: For states, by states.* Washington, DC: National Academies Press.

Partnership for Assessment of Readiness for College and Careers. (n.d.a). *PARCC training.* Accessed at http://parcctrng.testnav.com/client/index.html#login?username=PCPT15MT07PTEO0001&password=PCPRACTICE on August 12, 2016.

Partnership for Assessment of Readiness for College and Careers. (n.d.b). *Passage selection guidelines for the PARCC summative assessments, grades 3–11, in ELA/literacy.* Accessed at www.parcconline .org/files/186/ELA-Literacy%20Other%20Materials/609/passageselectionguidelines07_15.pdf on August 3, 2016.

Popham, W. J. (2003). *Test better, teach better: The instructional role of assessment.* Alexandria, VA: Association for Supervision and Curriculum Development.

Popham, W. J. (2007). All about accountability/grain size: The unresolved riddle. *Educational Leadership, 64*(8), 80–81.

Popham, W. J. (2008). *Transformative assessment.* Alexandria, VA: Association for Supervision and Curriculum Development.

Reeves, D. (2007). Challenges and choices: The role of educational leaders in effective assessment. In D. Reeves (Ed.), *Ahead of the curve: The power of assessment to transform teaching and learning* (pp. 227–251). Bloomington, IN: Solution Tree Press.

Rodriguez, M. C. (2005). Three options are optimal for multiple-choice items: A meta-analysis of 80 years of research. *Educational Measurement: Issues and Practice, 24*(2), 3–13.

Rothstein, D., & Santana, L. (2011). *Make just one change: Teach students to ask their own questions.* Cambridge, MA: Harvard Education Press.

Simon, S. (1988). *Volcanoes.* New York: HarperCollins.

Smarter Balanced Assessment Consortium. (n.d.a). *Development and design.* Accessed at www.smarterbalanced .org/smarter-balanced-assessments on December 29, 2015.

Smarter Balanced Assessment Consortium. (n.d.b). *Sample questions.* Accessed at www.smarterbalanced .org/assessments/sample-questions on April 4, 2016.

Smarter Balanced Assessment Consortium. (n.d.c). *Smarter Balanced grade 6 mathematics practice test scoring guide.* Accessed at www.southwindsorschools.org/uploaded/schools/TE/teams/evergreen /G6_Practice-Test_Student_Version_2015_AnswerKey.pdf on October 3, 2016.

Smarter Balanced Assessment Consortium. (2012a, April). *Issues related to stimulus and item development: A review of the current state of the field.* Accessed at http://citeseerx.ist.psu.edu/viewdoc/download;jsessionid=9DD72B39208CBF188BAF37753E752E16?doi=10.1.1.363.1314&rep=rep1&type=pdf on May 31, 2016.

Smarter Balanced Assessment Consortium. (2012b, April). *Mathematics item specifications grades 3–5.* Accessed at www.uidaho.edu/~/media/Files/Centers/CDA/ID%20Regional%20Math%20Center/Assessment/MathematicsGeneralItemandTaskSpecificationsGrades3-5.ashx on December 23, 2015.

Smarter Balanced Assessment Consortium. (2012c, April). *Performance task specifications.* Accessed at www.smarterbalanced.org/wp-content/uploads/2015/08/PerformanceTasksSpecifications.pdf on December 22, 2015.

Smarter Balanced Assessment Consortium. (2014). *Smarter Balanced scoring guide for selected short-text mathematics items (field test 2014).* Accessed at www.smarterbalanced.org/wp-content/uploads/2015/08/Smarter-Balanced-Scoring-Guide-for-Selected-Short-Text-Mathematics-Items.pdf on December 21, 2015.

Smarter Balanced Assessment Consortium. (2015a, April). *English language arts and literacy computer adaptive test (CAT) and performance task (PT) stimulus specifications.* Accessed at www.smarterbalanced.org/wp-content/uploads/2015/08/ELA-Stimulus-Specifications.pdf on December 23, 2015.

Smarter Balanced Assessment Consortium. (2015b, May 1). *Practice test scoring guide grade 6 mathematics.* Accessed at www.smarterbalanced.org/wp-content/uploads/2015/11/G6_Practice_Test_Scoring_Guide_Math.pdf on August 12, 2016.

Smarter Balanced Assessment Consortium. (2015c, May 1). *Practice test scoring guide grade 8 mathematics.* Accessed at www.smarterbalanced.org/wp-content/uploads/2015/11/G8_Practice_Test_Scoring_Guide_Math.pdf on August 12, 2016.

Stiggins, R. J., Arter, J. A., Chappuis, J., & Chappuis, S. (2004). *Classroom assessment* for *student learning: Doing it right—Using it well.* Portland, OR: Assessment Training Institute.

University of Arizona Institute for Mathematics and Education. (n.d.). *Progressions documents for the Common Core mathematics standards.* Accessed at http://math.arizona.edu/~ime/progressions on August 12, 2016.

University of Oregon. (n.d.). *UO DIBELS data system features.* Accessed at https://dibels.uoregon.edu/features on April 4, 2016.

Vagle, N. D. (2014). *Design in five: Essential phases to create engaging assessment practice.* Bloomington, IN: Solution Tree Press.

Webb, N. L. (1997). *Criteria for alignment of expectations and assessments in mathematics and science education* (Research monograph no. 8). Washington, DC: Council of Chief State School Officers.

West Virginia Board of Education. (n.d.). *WVBE content standards policies.* Accessed at https://wvde.state.wv.us/policies/csos.html on August 5, 2016.

Wiggins, G. (2012). Seven keys to effective feedback. *Educational Leadership, 70*(1), 10–16.

Wiliam, D. (2011). *Embedded formative assessment.* Bloomington, IN: Solution Tree Press.

Woodward, J., Beckmann, S., Driscoll, M., Franke, M., Herzig, P., Jitendra, A., et al. (2012, May). *Improving mathematical problem solving in grades 4 through 8: A practice guide* (NCEE 2012-4055). Washington, DC: National Center for Education Evaluation and Regional Assistance. Accessed at http://ies.ed.gov/ncee/wwc/pdf/practice_guides/mps_pg_052212.pdf on April 4, 2016.

INDEX

Common Formative Assessment
Kim Bailey and Chris Jakicic
Teams that engage in designing, using, and responding to common formative assessments are more knowledgeable about their own standards, more assessment literate, and able to develop more strategies for helping all students learn. In this conversational guide, the authors offer tools, templates, and protocols to incorporate common formative assessments into the practices of a PLC to monitor and enhance student learning.
BKF538

Collaborating for Success With the Common Core
Kim Bailey, Chris Jakicic, and Jeanne Spiller
Leverage teamwork to integrate the CCSS into your curriculum, and build on a foundational knowledge of PLCs. You'll gain a comprehensive understanding of the shifts required to implement the standards in core content areas and find valuable tips and strategies for creating strong collaborative practices. Identify the essential standards, determine learning targets, define proficiency, learn how to design rigorous assessments, and more.
BKF556

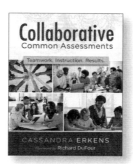

Collaborative Common Assessments
Cassandra Erkens
Foreword by Richard DuFour
Reignite the passion and energy assessment practices bring as tools to guide teaching and learning. Strengthen instructional agility in professional learning communities with collaborative common assessments that collect vital information and consider all levels of the organization. Explore the practical steps teacher teams must take to establish clear, comprehensive assessment systems, and discover how to continually improve results.
BKF605

The Teacher as Assessment Leader
Edited by Thomas R. Guskey
Meaningful examples, expert research, and real-life experiences illustrate the capacity and responsibility every educator has to ignite positive change. Packed with practical strategies for designing, analyzing, and using assessments, this book shows how to turn best practices into usable solutions.
BKF345

Learning by Doing, Third Edition
Richard DuFour, Rebecca DuFour, Robert Eaker, Thomas W. Many, and Mike Mattos
Discover how to transform your school or district into a high-performing PLC. The third edition of this comprehensive action guide offers new strategies for addressing critical PLC topics, including hiring and retaining new staff, creating team-developed common formative assessments, and more.
BKF746

Solution Tree | Press

a division of

Solution Tree

Visit SolutionTree.com or call 800.733.6786 to order.

"Excellent engagement
in what truly matters
in **assessment**.

Great examples!"

—Carol Johnson, superintendent,
Central Dauphin School District, Pennsylvania

🤝 PD Services

Our experts draw from decades of research and their own experiences to bring you practical strategies for designing and implementing quality assessments. You can choose from a range of customizable services, from a one-day overview to a multiyear process.

Book your assessment PD today!
888.763.9045

Solution Tree